"LOVE truly is the greatest gift from God that we can demonstrate to our spouse, but the second greatest is praying for them! *Loving Your Spouse Through Prayer* is one of the finest books you'll ever read. Cheri Fuller understands how very priceless, powerful, and life-changing this principle will be in your marriage as they are wholeheartedly joined together."

Dr. Gary and Barb Rosberg,
America's Family Coaches, nationally-known speakers and co-hosts of their own syndicated, daily radio program, authors of more than a dozen resources on marriage

"Marriage is challenging and more than ever needs to be covered in prayer. As you read this inspiring book by Cheri Fuller, you too will discover the blessing of praying God's Word for your spouse that will fill you with faith and hope, transform your spiritual life, and bring the life of Jesus and blessing into your marriage and family."

Dr. Archibald Hart and Dr. Catherine Hart Weber,
authors of *Stressed or Depressed, Unveiling Depression in Women* and *Secrets of Eve*

"Couples today face some unique challenges as they make decisions about jobs, family, children, finances . . . the worry and stress can be overwhelming. But, prayer can change everything. Cheri gives us a refreshing look at the power of prayer in marriage and how prayer can enable us to seek His will for guidance and establish grace-based communication. A must-read for every newly married to every seasoned married couple."

Dr. Tim Clinton,
President of The American Association of Christian Counselors and best-selling author of *Turn your Life Around*

loving

your spouse through

prayer

how to pray God's word into your marriage

CHERI FULLER

loving
your spouse through
prayer

how to pray God's word into your marriage

Published by
THOMAS NELSON
Since 1798

In order to preserve the privacy of the people involved,
names and aspects of their personal stories may have been changed.

LOVING YOUR SPOUSE THROUGH PRAYER

Published in association with the literary agency of Alive Communications, Inc., 7680 Goddard Street, Suite 200, Colorado Springs, Colorado, 80920.

Unless otherwise noted, Scriptures are taken from the HOLY BIBLE, NEW INTERNATIONAL VERSION®. Copyright © 1973, 1978, 1984 by International Bible Society. Used by permission of Zondervan Publishing House. All rights reserved.

Scriptures noted NLT are taken from the New Living Translation® (NLT®). Copyright © 1996. Used by permission of Tyndale House Publishers, Inc., Wheaton, Illinois 60189. All rights reserved.

Scriptures noted MSG are taken from *The Message.* Copyright © 1993, 1994, 1995, 1996, 2000, 2001, 2002. Used by permission of NavPress Publishing Group.

Scriptures noted NASB are taken from the NEW AMERICAN STANDARD BIBLE®. Copyright © 1960, 1962, 1963, 1971, 1972, 1973, 1975, 1977, 1995 by The Lockman Foundation. Used by permission.

"Blessed Be Your Name" was written by Matt and Beth Redman.

Cover Design: Brand Navigation
Interior Design: Susan Browne Design

ISBN-13: 978-0-7394-8004-5

Printed in the United States of America

In memory of my courageous, precious sister
Martha Heath Holland
December 31, 1942—April 22, 2006

contents

Acknowledgments

One of my favorite parts of writing a book is expressing thanks to those who are the unseen support and backbone of the project. Those who prayed are right at the top of that list! Heartfelt thanks to Peggy Stewart, Jo Hayes, Janet Page, Kathy Wirth, and Cynthia Tonn, Lisa Cronk, Kathy Coleman, Melina Shellenberger, Elaine Shaw, Anne Denmark, Carol Kent, Betsy West, Sandra Aldrich, Catherine Hart Weber, Melanie Hemry, Cindy McDowell, Susan Stewart, Cynthia Morris, Corrie Sargeant, Pam Whitley, Lindsey O'Conner, Heidi Brizendine, the AWSA women, and Lael Arrington. (Lael, your insightful feedback and encouragement in the home stretch meant the world!)

To the couples and women who allowed me to share their stories, many, many thanks! May you be blessed in your marriages and lives, more than you could ask for or think of.

Thank you to my agent, Lee Hough; Joey Paul, Kris Bearss, Jennifer Day, Scott Harris, and the brilliant team at Integrity Publishers; and especially Leslie Peterson, my editor. It is a privilege to work with you!

To my sons, Chris and Justin, and their wives, Maggie and Tiffany, thank you for prayers, encouragement, and cheering along the way. And thank you to Hans and the best and dearest daughter on the planet, Ali; all you did to care for our home and keep everything alive and going while I was away writing this summer is more deeply appreciated than you know!

Holmes, you get my biggest thanks of all. Not only are you an integral part of this book through our stories written here, but your faithful, ongoing prayers for me and for my writing and ministry and life mean the world to me. Thank you, honey, from the bottom of my heart for being God's gift to me and our family. And truly, the best is yet to be.

Prayer: The Best Love Language of All

For the word of God is full of living power.
HEBREWS 4:12 NLT

Marie raced into the house, put down the grocery bags, and sat down to get her breath. Seven months pregnant, she felt like a great, big, pink *Titanic*. She was crazy busy as a full-time event planner, a wife whose husband traveled out of the country half the time, and a mother to two active grade-school boys.

On the outside, this capable wife looked like she was handling everything: the event she was planning for former President Bush, the cookies for the school party, getting her boys to soccer on time. But on the inside, her heart raced just thinking about her schedule for that month, much less the family's upcoming move to Colorado and having a baby they hadn't planned while keeping up with her third-grader and fifth-grader's needs. Every night she fell into bed with a longer to-do list than she had when she got up.

She didn't want to burden her husband, Brad; he had enough on his plate and was leaving soon on another overseas business trip. When she was alone and the rest of the family was asleep, the inner conversations would begin: *I failed everybody again today. Everything was done less well than it deserved to be accomplished. The job got short shrift; the kids did too. And Brad . . . he gets the crumbs; forget about me.*

But nobody cares and nobody notices.

Day after day, it seemed her best just wasn't enough. That's why she was so anxious about this pregnancy. *This poor baby! I won't have one more ounce of energy for it*, she thought one day, unpacking the grocery bags and putting things away.

"When's dinner, Mom?" her older son yelled as he ran up the stairs.

"About thirty minutes!" she answered, bustling around the kitchen preparing stir-fry and setting the table. Though it was her birthday, she wasn't expecting anything. Her husband was a dear, loving guy, but not too good at remembering things like birthdays and anniversaries.

It wasn't that she missed the gifts so much (although they would have been wonderful); she just wanted to know she mattered to him. To her, finding and giving the perfect gift was part of saying, "I know you and appreciate you for who you are." But after fifteen years together (and a bunch of missed birthdays and anniversaries), she'd lowered her expectations to avoid another disappointment. Dinner and helping with the boys' homework as usual—that was the way it would be tonight too.

Twenty minutes later, Brad came in the door and the family gathered around the table for dinner. As Marie began picking up the dishes to put them in the sink, Brad said, "Honey, I want you to come in the living room with me and sit in the blue chair." When their boys started out to the basketball goal he said, "You guys come too."

Once there, he placed a wrapped package in her lap and then did something that amazed her. With their sons looking on, he laid his hands on her shoulders and began to pray Proverbs 31 over his wife, thanking God for her as he personalized the passage with her name:

Lord, thank you for my wife who's of such noble character.

Marie is worth more than rubies.

As her husband, I have full confidence in her

And because of her I lack nothing of value.

Thank you that she brings me good, not harm,

All the days of her life . . .

And gets up day after day, providing food for our family . . .

And sets about her work vigorously.

Her arms are strong for her tasks.

She sees that her work is profitable,

And her lamp does not go out at night...

My wife is clothed with strength and dignity;

She can laugh at the days to come.

How grateful we are that Marie speaks with wisdom

and faithful instruction is on her tongue.

She watches over the affairs of our household

And doesn't eat the bread of idleness. (see vv. 10–12, 15, 17–18, 25–27)

By the time Brad got to "Marie's children rise up and call her blessed; I do also, and I praise her" (see v. 28), she was crying the happiest of tears. As he prayed those words over her and thanked God for her, courage and joy welled up within her and fears dissolved. Those prayers made her feel more appreciated and loved than any gift he could have bought in a store. Not even jewelry, and she *loved* jewelry.

Brad wasn't demonstrative about his faith or big on praying aloud, so it meant even more. Through the gift of God's Word he prayed into Marie's life, he conveyed, "You are up to the challenge; you're not a failure. You are the love of my life." Nothing could have been more romantic. Nothing could have shown their sons more how their dad valued their mom as a woman, a mother, a faithful wife, and a productive and creative person.

And the package that sat in her lap? As lovely as it was, she doesn't even remember what was inside. But she's never forgotten how loved she felt when God's Word was prayed over her that night.

My husband and I, too, have found that praying biblical prayers for each other and our marriage is a way to invite God's blessing, power, and grace into our lives. Many years ago when we recommitted our lives to Christ and began a daily walk in his Word, I began praying biblical prayers for our marriage, for my husband Holmes' life, and for our children. And Holmes, in his own quiet way, did the same. Daily as I read the Bible, I'd notice a special verse and I'd put a date by it—"For Holmes, 5/88" or "For our marriage, 10/95." Then I'd write the verse on my current prayer card or in a journal and pray it, perhaps once or perhaps many times.

One of the first passages God led me to—as if he took a big highlighter and said, "This is what I want for Holmes"—was Psalm 1. So I wrote his name by it and over the years have prayed it scores of times for him: "Lord, may Holmes be a man who doesn't follow the advice of the wicked or stand around with mockers. Help him to delight in your Word, think about it, and meditate on it day and night—so he will be like a tree planted along the riverbank, bearing fruit in every season of his life. May his leaves never wither, and may he prosper in all he does" (see v. 1–3).

A few years later, in a search at the library to find the meaning of his name, I discovered *Holmes* means "from the river" or "with roots going into the river." I didn't know this at the time I began praying Psalm 1, but God knew my husband was going to go through trying times in his business life—and he wanted fruitfulness for him, and for his roots to sink deep into the soil of Christ's love, feed on the truth of Scripture, and drink from the river of Life. When Holmes later went through some hard years of financial droughts as a builder, I continued to pray Psalm 1 for him, and I continue to pray that his latter years will be even more productive and joyful than earlier years. I've seen the fruits of that prayer and God's faithfulness as in his late fifties Holmes has come into his own, using his talents and gifts in architectural consulting with great productivity in ways we'd never imagined.

Do you know I've never run out of prayers to pray for my husband and marriage? "Let your word be a lamp for Holmes' feet and a light for his path" (see Psalm 119:105) hit the target when he changed jobs and needed direction in 1978. When he needed strength after a cross-country move in the eighties my desire was, "May your glorious unlimited resources give Holmes mighty inner strength through your Spirit" (see Ephesians 3:16). On another day and year I was struck by Colossians 1:9–10, put my husband's and my initials by it in my Bible, and wrote in my journal, "Lord, make us wise with spiritual wisdom and understanding of what you want to do in our lives so the way we live will honor and please you and we'll know you better and better." In Proverbs—oh, there were many verses in Proverbs I prayed for Holmes—I found the hope that Holmes would "experience all the riches of God's wisdom and knowledge" (see 9:10) and prayed that he would "trust in the Lord with all his heart and not lean on his own understanding" (Proverbs 3:5).

Sometimes the finger pointed right at me! As I read 1 Peter 3:4 and discovered how important it was to have a "gentle and quiet spirit" that was "quick to listen" (James 1:19) instead of talking so much (I was far from all this and knew it would take a big work of God), I wrote my name by those words and asked to be transformed. I've prayed many a "Create in me a clean heart (toward my mate and others I interact with today)" prayer (see Psalm 51:10). And a precious friend like Flo Perkins encouraged me to pray 1 Peter 4:8—that God would grant me the love that "covers a multitude of sins" when I was disappointed with my spouse or myself.

Holmes has prayed biblical prayers for me as well, including Proverbs 31. When I've had a lot going on—a book, article, or message to write—he has prayed that my mind would be renewed (see Romans 12:2) and that I'd have the mind of Christ and experience God's presence and voice in a deeper way and not be distracted by the "little foxes"—things of the world that would interfere with what God intends to do through me (see Song of Solomon 2:15). Many times he has prayed that I'd be refreshed as I minister to others in speaking and writing (Proverbs 11:25). And lately he asked me to pray that he'd experience life and wisdom in God's Word.

John Piper said that our general prayers "become powerful when they are filled up with concrete, radical biblical goals for the people we are praying for."[1] Holmes and I just passed thirty-seven years together by the grace of God, and after praying hundreds and hundreds of biblical prayers through those years, and having been the recipient of countless prayers by my husband, I've been filled with faith instead of doubt and fear, in the best of times and the most difficult of seasons. Time after time that faith has given me more hope for my husband and those I was praying for. And now we're praying biblical prayers for our two sons and daughter and their spouses and marriages as well.

Praying God's Word transformed my spiritual life and did something else: it got my focus off me, my husband, and the problems or situations and onto the One who could help us, transform us, and, when needed, restore us. I knew it wasn't an overnight quick fix, but my confidence in the Lord increased as I grew to trust him to fulfill my petitions in his way and on his timetable. And I was assured—even when the answers were long in coming—that he who said he is able to keep safe what we entrust to him will do more than we can ask, think, or imagine, because of his riches in glory in Christ Jesus (see Ephesians 3:20–21).

Like Marie and Brad experienced and like we have discovered, you, too, can find the blessing of praying God's Word for your spouse and your life together. The words we speak about our spouse and marriage are powerful and have influence and impact. James 3 says there is life or death in the power of the tongue and that we can curse or bless with our words (v. 10). When we pray God's words and love our husband or wife through prayer, we breathe life—the life of Jesus, the living Word—into the marriage. Who among us doesn't need more of Christ in our lives and his blessing in our family?

You may be wondering, *Why pray God's Word into my marriage when I've already got a lot of things to ask God for? I know what we need. What's so great about praying Bible prayers?* If so, consider this: because his thoughts and ways are different and higher than ours, the Lord has given us the treasure of his Word to guide and shape our prayers, to discover what he wants for our marriage, family, and all areas of our life. Even more, not just when we read it, but when we *pray* his Word into our marriage, we are asking that all he's planned in heaven would come into our lives on earth. We're agreeing with what he wants.

St. Augustine once blamed himself for all the lost time trying to find God's will when, from the very beginning, he could have done so by praying the Word.[2] His Word can guide us, too. My friend Jennifer Dean shared in her book *Heart's Cry: Principles of Prayer* about a time in her marriage when her relationship with her husband, Wayne, was strained. She was frustrated and felt unable to pray. One morning God spoke to her as she was reading in Jeremiah: "I will give [you and Wayne] singleness of heart and action, so that [you] will always fear me for [your] own good and the good of [your] children after [you]" (Jeremiah 32:39). She recognized God was showing her his heart and desire for her marriage and she agreed with his will by praying this. She no longer had to try to convince herself that God would work. He told her so himself, and it was not long until he began to bring his Word to pass and bring her and Wayne into a unity of heart and action.[3]

The true stories you will read in the pages ahead demonstrate the power of God's Word and prayer in not only my and Holmes's lives but the lives of some very unique couples in different situations and seasons of their marriage. Let me encourage you that despite our best efforts, whether you've been married a year or twenty-five years, every one of our marriages needs prayer. There's hardly a marriage on the planet that doesn't come under spiritual attack or endure trying times. Many marriages are in deep trouble today in our nation. Two people in a broken world who pledge themselves "till death do us part" face all kinds of challenges to harmony—their own differences and selfishness or perhaps pain from their wounded childhoods. Situations such as chronic illness, the loss of a child, financial failures, burnout, and time pressures may tear at the fabric of their relationship.

But here's the good news: when we call out to God on behalf of our spouse, when we pray God's Word into our marriage, "on the other end of that prayer line is a loving heavenly father who has promised to hear and answer our petitions. In this day of disintegrating families on every side, we dare not try to make it on our own," said Dr. James Dobson.[4]

With that in mind, after each story in this book we begin a journey of self-discovery with a section titled "Heart to Heart: Questions for Reflection, Discussion, and Journaling" so you can interact with God or your spouse about the issues that hit home. There's even room to write your own Marriage Prayers. (These sections are excellent resources for small-group discussion, too.)

Then, coming through to the other side of that introspection, you'll find our "Glimpses of God" section, where I'll share with you a quality or facet of God reflected through the marriage story and the scriptural foundation of that part of God's nature. While writing this book, I saw over and over little glimpses of God's faithfulness as I heard from other husbands and wives: how he's the God of restoration, the God of second chances, the God who provides for a husband and wife, the God who gives a future and a hope when there seems none, the God whose peace is the hallmark of a couple who trusts him with all their hearts—no matter what they go through.

It reminds me of what Oswald Chambers once said—that God doesn't always tell us what he is going to do; he reveals *who he is*.[5]

When God created marriage, he designed the relationship between husband and wife to give us a deeper understanding of who he is. And as Pastor Jack Arrington said, "When their relationship is functioning as it was designed, their relationship of love teaches us something of what God is like."[6] Or, as Paul said it in Ephesians 5:22–33, the marriage relationship is to model and reflect the relationship of Jesus Christ, the Bridegroom, with his Bride, the church.

So, make use of these Glimpses of God—they are like a breath of fresh air as we pause to collect our thoughts and remember God is an awesome God regardless of our own shortcomings. In remembering this we are renewed and refreshed as we begin a new chapter and a new journey of self-discovery.

Finally, note there is a whole section of "Topical Prayers for Your Marriage and Mate" at the end of the book that contains some special prayers to bless your marriage.

In utilizing all these sections, my desire is that through the pages of this book you'll gain much hope for your marriage and that you'll be inspired to pray God's Word for your husband or wife and the couples who come behind you. That you'll be encouraged by the stories to the point you will delve into the treasure trove of biblical prayers—for your own marriage—that are right at your fingertips in the Bible. The Word of God is alive and powerful. May it jumpstart your prayers and energize your spiritual life day after day! May you give the gift of God's Word to your spouse again and again. And may you both be blessed beyond your wildest dreams, to God's glory.

Living with Genuine Affection

Chapter One

Love each other with a genuine affection.

ROMANS 12:10 NLT

The *ticktock* of the wall clock, usually rhythmic and soothing, seemed to resound like Big Ben in the confines of our family room. Holmes sat across the room in his burgundy leather easy chair, glasses perched on his nose, reading a five-hundred-page history book while I sat curled on the sofa perusing *Writers' Digest* magazine and making notes for the writer's critique group I was teaching the next day. I couldn't focus on my work for glancing over at Holmes and listening to the silence.

When had we stopped talking and begun to feel so alone together?

It wasn't one of those comfortable silences born of intimacy. It had happened so gradually that neither of us seemed to notice.

I glanced out the window and saw a wild red fox at the feeder Holmes had set up in the trees on the back of our acre lot.

"Holmes, look who's come up from the woods and is back at the feeder!"

Holmes looked over his specs as a slow smile crossed his face. "It looks like we've fattened him up a bit, don't you think?"

"I do," I agreed as we watched the animal scamper off into the woods.

"Thanks for pointing him out," Holmes said. "I enjoy watching him."

"You're welcome."

Holmes gazed out the window for a few moments before return-
ing to his book. Several silent hours later we went to bed. At almost the same instant we each reached over to turn off our bedside
lamps. Backs to one another, we each said, "Good night."

When had we stopped snuggling?

How long had it been since we'd talked in the dark until sleep
overtook us? How long since Holmes had reached for my hand, put
his arm around me in the movie theater, or really looked into my
eyes? It scared me that I couldn't remember.

He snored quietly while I lay in the dark long after midnight wondering when we'd become polite strangers and if it was possible to
find what we'd lost.

We hadn't always been like this. There were times of great fun
as a family when the kids were growing up and special memories of
traveling together, which we both enjoyed. But a long, suffocating
series of setbacks had left Holmes depressed and void of energy. The
sparkle had simply gone out of his eyes. It didn't help that his job
seemed to be heading toward a dead end. He was already worrying
about what we'd do for income then. (We were praying for a new
job, and he had been looking but hadn't found one.) Living under a
high degree of stress and crushing financial pressures as we had for
so long had drained our marriage of joy like the air that leaks slowly
out of a balloon.

"Affection is responsible for nine-tenths
of whatever solid and durable happiness
there is in our lives." C. S. Lewis

I was really good at pep talks, like "Honey, let's communicate more. Let's go out of town this weekend. Maybe a change of scenery would do us good."

"I'm tired," he'd reply. "I'm going to bed early."

"Want to go on a walk with me and wind up at the Morrises' to visit?" I might ask after dinner. But he had no energy for a stroll or interest in being with friends. Since he'd said more than his daily quota of words at work, all he wanted to do was collapse in a chair and bury himself in a book or a football game on TV until sleep overtook him.

Little conversation. Less intimacy. And often the tension between us was palpable. When two people are in pain, I've found the ache seems to increase when they're together.

But I have to be honest here—*I* was a big part in what had become our dry, unaffectionate marriage. You've probably already guessed that. As my mother used to say, "It takes two to tango" when there's a relationship problem or conflict. And there was *plenty* in the "my part" category. For starters, without realizing it, I was mad as all get out. An underlying anger had simmered within me for mistakes that had put us in financial peril. I'd forgiven and forgiven. But still . . .

And too, in times like these that were so stressful, I felt emotionally abandoned by his silence and "move away" behavior. We loved each other and were committed to each other "till death do we part," but I was frankly depleted and getting depressed myself. For someone who loves being with people and going places together, living with my precious walking-zombie husband had become isolating and lonely. I tried to bury myself in my work, but the truth is I longed for a closer relationship with my husband of thirty-five years.

One morning, sitting on the sun porch where I always start the day with coffee, my Bible, and God (not necessarily in that order), I read Romans 12:10 in *The One Year Bible*. The morning light came in, filtered by the multicolored, antique stained-glass window. And I was struck by the simplicity and power of Paul's words: "Love each other with genuine affection, and take delight in honoring each other" (NLT).

This was *so* not our marriage. It was convicting. It wasn't just a nice idea or spiritual concept—it was exactly what my heart was longing for, and what we needed desperately in our marriage: *to love each other with a genuine affection.*

As I delved into the verse, I searched on the Internet dictionaries to ponder the word *affection*. On my first attempt at Googling the word, a dictionary web site tried to send me to Match.com to "explore the science of love" and find my new soul mate. Things were tough, but this was not exactly what I had in mind.

In another thesaurus I found synonyms of the word *affection*: *warmhearted* (we certainly needed to warm up toward each other), *tender* (trying a little tenderness surely wouldn't hurt), *cherishing, loving, fondness, a sentimental or protective affection.* Now we were getting somewhere.

I got onto my knees on the rug. *Oh, Lord, we need you to restore affection. This is what we need in our marriage! Please forgive me for my coldness toward Holmes.*

I thought about the times I'd stayed busy at my computer when Holmes walked in from work instead of giving him a hug. The nights I'd been "too tired" to make love when he was probably longing for physical closeness. The times I'd wanted him to put his arm around me in the movie theatre but his hand was in the popcorn bag for two hours. I was desperate for God to do something.

Dissolve my anger and replace it with forgiveness. Please change our hearts and teach us to really love each other with a genuine affection.

In our own ways we had each pushed the other away. How was God going to reconnect us? I was so drained and depleted that I knew no amount of self-effort was going to fix things.

Then I remembered the truth that nothing is impossible with God. I wrote the verse down on a 3x5 card that reminds me to pray specifically for certain people and tucked it in my Bible. Day after day, Romans 12:10 resounded in my heart. Morning after morning I brought it to God. He heard about our desperate need for affection over and over and over throughout that month and the weeks that followed. Early mornings on the sun porch. When I was driving. Walking my thirty minutes a day. I'd pause and lift our need to God: *Lord, please love my husband through me. Fill me up with your amazing love for him and let it flow to him.*

Not that anything changed overnight. External stresses increased in the next weeks, and Holmes retreated to his "cave," but something in me wouldn't give up. God made me about as persistent as the widow in Luke 18:1–6 who went to the judge in her city asking repeatedly for justice, the story says, even though the judge ignored her for a while. Day after day, he turned her away. But finally, because "this woman is driving me crazy" (v. 5 NLT), the judge said, he granted her request.

I knew God was a lot more gracious than the uncaring judge. So even on days when things looked grim and we were anything but huggy-huggy, I kept on asking.

The more I prayed this verse, the more little rays of hope began to glimmer within me. One day the thought occurred to me, What if Holmes and I really started doing this? *What if all husbands and wives treated each other with a sincere, affectionate love?* How happy God would be about that. And what a role model we'd be to our married children and the watching world.

"Love must be learned again and again; there is no end to it."

Katherine Anne Porter

At first nothing happened on the outside or in the state of our marital bliss. But a few months later, in July, God answered our prayer for a new job for Holmes. Trouble was it was *four hours away* from where we live.

So suddenly my husband was transplanted to another city. I took care of the cat, the house, and my work while he worked in Dallas and lived with relatives. Since it was a temporary consulting job, we couldn't pull up stakes and move. We didn't have the money to move anyway.

This was *not* how I had thought the Lord would answer my prayer, but then he reminded me that his ways aren't our ways.

"How are you doing?" my friend Cynthia asked a few days after Holmes had left, knowing that this was the first time in thirty-six years of marriage for Holmes and me to live apart (except when he served in the National Guard in the seventies).

"Well, to tell you the truth, it's like the dark cloud moved south," I answered. Although I missed my husband's presence at the dinner table and all the things he did to keep things running smoothly around the house, it was a little like an emotional break for both of us. The atmosphere in our house was lighter somehow.

I stayed busy with our two grandkids, Noah and Luke, who live down the street; leading a prayer group for mothers of college and career kids; and writing assignments. It was really different making meals for one; I've never been fond of eating alone. Sleeping alone at night wasn't my favorite thing either. I missed Holmes' warm body beside me as I read myself to sleep. But the week went fast, and by the end I was watching the street for his car to turn in the drive.

That first Friday night, Holmes stepped in the door with a bouquet of flowers for me. It wasn't my birthday or a special occasion. It was my quiet husband's way of expressing himself.

Yellow roses one week, pink carnations another Friday night, white daisies and tulips, asters and peonies. Being a lover of flowers, week by week those Friday night bouquets began to melt my heart.

I-35 became our Main Street. And though he was tired from a week of long, twelve-hour days of work and the four-hour commute home, Holmes realized we only had an abbreviated time together—since he had to leave again on Sunday evening—so he made an extra effort to communicate and relate to me in a meaningful way in the two days we had together. It seemed he had missed me too.

And instead of talking about problems or the mounds of business and bills we had to take care over the weekend, I met him with a huge hug and one of his favorite meals—meat loaf and mashed potatoes. I made a point to ask him what was new at the development company he worked for and to really listen instead of launching off into another issue the way I sometimes did.

Since he was in a job that utilized his gifts and talents better than any position in the last ten years, he was in better spirits, his

Connecting and Rekindling Affection in Your Marriage

• *Plan a getaway together.* It doesn't have to be flying to a Florida beach for the weekend (although that would be wonderful!). A change of scenery can do wonders to stir up loving feelings. If you have kids at home, trade baby-sitting night or weekends with friends and watch for specials at a local bed-and-breakfast. It doesn't have to be fancy, but getting away together can help the sparks catch fire again.

• *Leave a love note.* Besides sending loving e-mail notes, include a note in your spouse's lunch bag occasionally or inside her suitcase to be found on a trip. Mail a sweet note to his workplace. Make it short and sincere, and include something you love or appreciate about him. You'll bless his socks off.

• *Make connecting with your spouse a priority.* What helps you connect as a couple? One way I've found is what I call "getting on your mate's turf." Find something he or she really enjoys and do it together. If it's golf, drive the cart on a summer evening and enjoy the sunset together at the end of nine holes. Watch an NFL football game together. Read to each other. Go out for breakfast on Saturday morning or to Barnes & Noble for coffee. Play Scrabble or Hearts, do a crossword puzzle, or take a walk together. The goal of the activity is to connect—and engaging in something fun or enjoyable smoothes the way.

• *Create an atmosphere.* Maybe like ours, your bedroom is full of magazines or the bedside table is jam-packed with books. A bag from a shopping trip, suitcases you haven't unpacked, and other assorted clutter block the view. Make your bedroom a place of beauty and peace—as much as is possible. I found even small changes like lighting a candle on the bedside table can make a difference.

If you need more ideas to warm up your marriage, read one of Dave and Claudia Arps' *10 Great Dates* books, which are full of easy, fun ideas to put sizzle back in your relationship.[2]

self-worth boosted. And I had a renewed appreciation for all the *many* things he did to keep the house and lawn and cars running—especially now that I was doing a lot of them by myself.

We slowly, little by little, began to reconnect and enjoy one another again. On our Saturday-night movie dates. Savoring little bits of quiet time together over breakfast on the sun porch. Spending part of Saturday afternoon at Barnes & Noble.

"Be absolutely certain that the Lord loves you, devotedly and individually, loves you just as you are." *Abbe Henri de Tourville*

And in the midst of those moments, God was there, showing up again and again.

The pressures and stress in our life didn't decrease. In fact, the very next month our son's orders were changed and he and his battalion were sent to the combat zone in Iraq. Chris, a Navy doctor, went into the deadly front lines of the battle of Fallujah to care for wounded Marines.

Over the years, couple prayer had been a part of our life together. We'd prayed when our kids were sick or had school problems or needed good friends when they moved to a new school. We'd even prayed some girlfriends out the door.

But having a son in a war was like nothing we'd experienced. Like the day we heard on the news that a helicopter had crashed, killing all the Marines and medical personnel aboard, and one of those men was named Lt. Chris Fuller. It wasn't until hours later we found out our Chris Fuller was safe.

For the agonizing nine months our son was in Iraq, the target of snipers, IEDs, and rocket-propelled mortars, we prayed on the phone night after night for Chris and the Marines he served as battalion surgeon. And with every prayer God reconnected our hearts together a little more. We realized more than ever how important it was to unite and agree in prayer rather than rely on our own separate prayer efforts when our son—or anybody else we knew—was in harm's way.

As a little side benefit of his new job, Holmes learned to use a computer, and e-mail became a new way to relay our thoughts to each other. Love notes would pop up in my inbox: "I miss you." "Can't wait to see you Friday night. Love you, H." I'd send him loving messages via the Internet as well. Slowly the home fires began to burn again as emotional, physical, and spiritual intimacy began to weave together. Just as spring follows winter, closeness and affection were restored to our life together. And I've never ceased to thank God for rekindling the flame in our marriage.

From time to time I still pray that prayer from Romans 12:10, not only for our own marriage, but for our three married children and their spouses. And others outside the family too. Every couple undergoes stresses and strains on their marriage that can dampen affection—all the way from a new baby; prolonged illness in husband, wife, or child; financial reversals; moving. . . . But there's always hope for rekindling the flame. Praying this Scripture is the place to start.

Heart to Heart:

Questions for Reflection, Discussion, and Journaling

1. *What's the roadblock?* Is unforgiveness or anger blocking affection and love in your marriage? What are everyday things that trigger your anger?

2. According to marriage experts, unforgiveness, resentment, and bitterness act as roadblocks to intimacy and affection in a marriage. If you're angry at your spouse because he/she has hurt you, that's nothing to be ashamed about. But note this wonderful advice in Ephesians on handling it so it doesn't damage your marriage or other relationships: "You do well to be angry—but don't use your anger as fuel for revenge. And don't stay angry. Don't go to bed angry. Don't give the Devil that kind of foothold in your life" (Ephesians 4:26 Message). Have you had trouble letting go of anger? If so, what happened?

3. *Burnout: the affection buster.* Another obstacle to affection is living in a constant state of overdrive, overcommitment, and exhaustion. Doctors and researchers say more than thirty million women have "hurried-woman syndrome."[1] It's tough for overbooked, overstretched, exhausted, burned-out individuals to connect emotionally or physically. We're just too tired to even *think* a romantic

thought. Ever been there? Things like learning to say no if you're overscheduled, planning some free time, and practicing simplicity can help. What could you do to reevaluate your commitments and cut back to relieve the constant exhaustion? How could you refuel and take time for some R and R so you have energy for your marriage instead of giving it the crumbs?

4. It's not a quick fix and may take counseling and time, but you can find freedom from unforgiveness, anger, and other roadblocks to affection. Recall and share about a time God brought freedom to your heart or gave you a fresh start in your relationship.

5. *"These are a few of my favorite things . . ."* What is one way you could show affection to your spouse this week? What are some of your husband's or wife's favorite things, whether that's an activity to do together, a favorite meal, a back rub, or a small gift that would speak volumes? Is there a tangible need you could meet so he or she could experience your caring? To stir your thinking, check out the sidebar "Connecting and Rekindling Affection in Your Marriage."

Your Own Marriage Prayer

Based on Romans 12:10, write out a prayer for your relationship that expresses your deepest desires and what you want God to do in reconnecting you emotionally, spiritually, and physically in this season of life together. Perhaps you want to pray for creativity in nurturing a connection or showing love.

Glimpses of God: A God of Affection

God isn't a cold or distant God. The Bible describes him as a God of great affection who exults over us with joy, who quiets us with his love and rejoices over us with shouts of joy (see Zephaniah 3:17). That's pretty enthusiastic love! His love toward his children is as high as the heavens are above the earth (see Psalm 103:11). He loves us with tenderness, generosity, and an intimacy that's beyond our wildest dreams.

Because you belong to him and before the foundation of the earth were part of him, God says, "Can a woman forget her nursing child, and have no compassion on the son of her womb? Even these may forget, but I will not forget you. Behold, I have inscribed you on the palms of my hands" (Isaiah 49:15–16, NASB). As someone once said, "God carries your picture in his wallet."

He also loves your spouse this way. Maybe you feel you're fresh out of love for him or her and have no romantic feelings right now. You aren't sure if you even like him. If so, I have some wonderful news for you: God hasn't run out of love for your spouse. He knows his past and his future and even the thoughts he tries to hide, and he still loves him. No matter what he has done or not done, the Lord has an inexhaustible supply of love we can tap into. And it's unconditional love, not based on performance or personal goodness. You don't have to muster it up yourself. You don't have to pretend and put on a loving, happy face if you're not feeling it.

You can make an honest confession like, "God, I'm not feeling loving," "I don't feel anything for him," or "My well of love has just run dry." Be real. He knows your heart and thoughts anyway. Then you can ask the Lord to love your mate through you and shed abroad his love in your heart through the Holy Spirit, with words like, "But God, you are full of love and affection, and I know you love my husband (or wife). Give me your love and affection for him (or her). Let it flow through me." Then be ready to experience a new kind of love.

Gratitude:
The Heart of Prayer

Chapter Two

*Keep on praying. No matter what happens, always
be thankful, for this is God's will for you who
belong to Christ Jesus. . . . Tell God what you need,
and thank him for all he has done.*

1 Thessalonians 5:17–18 nlt,
Philippians 4:6 nlt

"Honey, I'm home! And I've got great news!" Randy called as he rushed through the door into the kitchen where his wife of eighteen years was preparing dinner.

"Don't keep me in suspense. What's up?" Valerie asked as her husband gave her a big hug.

"I've been promoted! It's just what I've been working for and hoping for. The only hitch was my boss gave me two hours to make the decision. But I thought about what a great opportunity it was, so I said yes. We'll be relocating to Victorville and get to buy a big new house. Isn't it terrific?"

Instead of sharing her husband's enthusiasm, Valerie's face fell.

"What's wrong, Val? Don't you think this is great?"

"Besides the fact that you didn't ask my opinion before you made the decision, I don't really want to move. I don't want a new house. I love this one. And how can we take Rachel out of the ballet program and gifted programs she's in at the high school, besides our church and all our friends?" she asked.

"We'll find another church and Rachel can get into great programs in her new high school," he encouraged. "The changes we have to make are worth it for this promotion."

"You know we don't have to sell the house to buy one in Victorville," Valerie told Randy. "I'll be okay about moving as long as you don't sell the house. A missionary couple or somebody from church can rent it. But let's not sell it."

They ended up compromising for the short term. While Valerie stayed in San Diego for Rachel to finish out her daughter's school year, her husband went to Victorville to start his new job. But as the weeks went on, Valerie knew there was one thing she could not give up: the house they'd purchased with the proceeds of two houses she'd owned before the marriage. Having been part of a military family and moving frequently during her growing-up years made this house all the more important to Valerie. It was the home they were going to raise not only their children in but have their grandkids come to. And she'd given everything she owned in earthly goods to buy it.

Every time they talked about the "to sell or not to sell" issue they were at each other's throats; they couldn't agree about anything, which meant continual conflict. They weren't even close to the same page regarding what should be done. Additionally, they lived in different places and although they'd pledged themselves to each other years ago at the altar, they weren't in agreement in their decisions about their kids.

"What a grand world would it be if we could forget our troubles as easily as we forget our blessings." *Unknown*

Finally, in spite of her objections, Randy put their home on the market. He wouldn't pray with his wife about it. He knew what she thought. He just made an executive decision and sold it.

The family moved to Apple Valley and Valerie continued to struggle with anger toward her husband. Especially when she saw the property values in San Diego push the prices of homes upward and their old house tripled in value within the year. And it wasn't just the financial mistake she resented. It went far deeper.

If I have no value in the marriage, if I put everything into it and he ignores me and my opinions, what's the point? Why should I even care about our marriage?

To add to the stress, their daughter, Rachel, began having problems. Though she'd been the model student in the other city, she exploded like a bomb in the new high school. She couldn't find a youth group she fit into. There was no ballet program, no enrichment or challenge at her new school. When she went out for cheerleading and made the team, a group of girls beat her severely because they were jealous. Finally, at the end of her rope with her own struggles and her parents' adversarial relationship, Rachel reached the verge of suicide. She wrote her mother a letter: "Mom, I need help."

Valerie's heart ached for her daughter. She and Randy found a counselor to help her, and thankfully things eventually improved with Rachel.

But the marriage was going downhill. There was a strain between Randy and Valerie that wouldn't go away.

When I met Valerie after a session I taught at a women's conference on the power of praying as a couple, she told me her husband had no interest in prayer. She listed some of his other imperfections and mistakes, like selling their San Diego house. He went to church and Promise Keepers, but they had no real prayer life together, Valerie told me. Even when someone they knew was in great need, when she'd ask, "Could we pray?" Randy would answer, "Go for it," and be silent.

"Look, Val, I don't pray out loud because I'm afraid my language isn't good enough to God," Randy said when she tried to talk to him about it.

She tried giving him suggestions like praying the Psalms. Getting several different books to try to get her husband to pray didn't work. She'd even spent an hour leading him through the four steps of prayer and teaching him to pray in one accord like they did in her Moms In Touch group. That just overwhelmed him and frustrated her even more when he wouldn't join in.

"It was more like I was the teacher, and he really backed off after that one, making excuses to avoid praying with me," Valerie explained. Long prayers just went against his grain. It didn't help that Randy had vertigo, so if he stood with his head bowed and eyes closed, he got dizzy and nauseated as his wife dumped out the whole backpack of her worries: their daughter, finances, her family, her residual pain from a car accident.

And it definitely didn't increase his desire to pray with his wife when her prayers were peppered with admonitions like, "Lord, help Randy be more of the spiritual leader in our home instead of watching so much ESPN."

As Randy resisted his wife's spiritual direction and abdicated his role as prayer leader, their son filled the gap, taking over the man's spot in the house when company came and a dinner prayer was in order. That worked for a while—until he graduated from high school and eventually got married and moved away. Then the burden shifted back to Valerie.

"Gratitude unlocks the fullness of life.
It turns what we have into enough, and
more. It turns denial into acceptance,
chaos to order, confusion to clarity. It can
turn a meal into a feast, a house into a
home, a stranger into a friend. Gratitude
makes sense of our past, brings peace for
today, and creates a vision for tomorrow."

Melody Beattie

"Is there *any* time your husband is willing to pray with you?" I asked.

"Just mealtime."

"That's a great place to begin. I want you to start by thanking God for something specific about your husband," I encouraged. "And in your own devotional time, pray this prayer from 1 Thessalonians 5:18, asking the Lord to give you a grateful spirit and for you to become one with your husband again."

"But you don't understand how frustrated I am with him!" Valerie said, listing her litany of complaints about her husband again. I gently pointed that out to her, along with noting their conflict over the house seemed to overshadow any of Randy's good qualities. And surely he had some good qualities!

That had never occurred to Valerie. But she'd tried everything else and was close to the end of her rope, so it was worth a try. The first night home after the conference, it was her turn as usual to say the prayer of thanks before dinner. Instead of jabbing Randy by talking about the rising real estate prices in their old neighborhood as she often did, she bowed her head and said, "Lord, thank you for all Randy's hard work and how if he comes home and I've had a bad day, he does whatever's needed without a word."

His mouth almost dropped open from surprise.

The next night she said, "Father, thank you for how thoughtful Randy was today to call and see if we needed milk, bread, or anything on his way home."

"Lord, thank you for Randy's perseverance, that even when he's sick, he still goes to work to provide for us so generously and helps me when my pain level is high," went Wednesday's prayer.

"Jesus, thank you for how Randy fixed the towel rack that had fallen down. When he sees a need, he just quietly helps. I'm so grateful for him."

For the first time in their twenty-two years of marriage, Randy gradually began to move *toward* his wife when she asked him to pray instead of running in the opposite direction.

"There is a calmness to a life lived in gratitude, a quiet joy." *Ralph H. Blum*

Quietly, mysteriously, the power of God's Word and prayer began to transform their marriage. Slowly the old resentments dissolved and Valerie's anger dissipated as she realized her husband had done his part several months before—admitting his mistake in selling their San Diego home without her being in agreement about it. Now it was up to her to let it go and forgive. As forgiveness flowed, Valerie experienced more freedom to love her husband and enjoy

29 Things I Love about . . .

A fun thing to do for a birthday or anniversary gift is to write on lovely

bordered paper a list of things you appreciate about your spouse. For

instance, if you've been married to Dan for twenty-nine years, you'd

create a list called "29 Things I Love about Dan." If your wife, Kate,

is celebrating her thirty-fifth birthday, you'd create a list entitled "35

Things I Love about Kate." It's a great way to stir up your own sense

of gratitude for your mate and to express it in a memorable way.

him than she'd felt for a long time. She discovered that every day came with its own gifts and she could untie the ribbons with gratefulness.

They also grew to be more in agreement on household decisions than they'd been in years. Even their kids noticed the new harmony when they came home from college. And when Randy's brother was in a terrible accident and lay in ICU for six days, his skull fractured and his lungs punctured, they were able to pray together for him as never before.

"Help us to help others."

"Lord, please help Rick in his healing; give the doctors wisdom and help the blood dissipate from his brain."

"Bless our children in their college courses."

"Thank you, Father, for such a faithful husband."

"Thank you, God, for my wife."

Randy and Valerie slowly became the partners in prayer she'd always hoped they would be, as the power of gratefulness transformed their marriage and spiritual life. Today, for the first time in twenty-five years of marriage, Randy is leading and teaching a small-group Bible study.

Heart to Heart:
QUESTIONS FOR REFLECTION, DISCUSSION, AND JOURNALING

1. *Choosing thankfulness.* Gratitude is the awareness that God is the source of all the gifts in our lives—most important, the gift of life itself. Besides being the heart of prayer, gratefulness is also one of the secrets to a fulfilled life as a couple.

Marriage is a gift; our spouse and children are gifts. Today is a gift. But we are often so focused on the problems, we forget to acknowledge the precious gifts we've already been given. As Rabbi Harold S. Kushner said, "Instead of wishing that your mate could read your mind and fulfill all of your wishes, be humbly grateful that there is someone in the world to love you and put up with your quirks."[1] We saw what happened when gratefulness replaced criticism in Randy and Valerie's life. What do you think might change in your own marriage if you took the same path?

2. Often our present stress causes us to focus on the problems instead of the positive things in our lives. And when we want something in our husband or wife to change, we often use prayer as a pep talk for self-improvement: "Lord, help him make it a priority to spend time with you instead of watching so much television" or "Father, give her more patience with the kids." Think: what do you appreciate about your spouse? Write it here.

The next time you sit down to pray, whether at the breakfast table or in bed late at night, consider thanking God for some of these specific things about your spouse.

3. *No strings attached.* However big or small the comment, expressing appreciation to God within hearing range of your spouse can do more than a hundred sermons to open his or her heart. Especially if it's in a no-strings-attached attitude—not to manipulate but just to express gratefulness and give credit where credit is due.

If you currently have a hard time thinking of things to thank God for about your spouse, jog your memory here by starting a list of qualities or character traits you loved about him or her *before* you got married:

4. *View your mate in a positive light.* Spouses live up or down to our beliefs about them. When a marriage runs into troubled waters—or dry ground—continual disappointments or conflict lead to seeing each other in a negative way. They pick up our negative attitude toward them and often act in accordance with our lowered expectations, perpetuating the frustration. Writing positive things

about your spouse can be a powerful assignment. Mark Goldstein, a psychologist, gave a group of couples on the brink of divorce one assignment: to go home and write all the positive things their partners did through the next week. The result? Seventy percent of the couples who did this reported major improvement in marital satisfaction.[2]

After taking five minutes a day to note positive things about your mate, write the results you experience:

Going a step further and letting your mate hear you thanking God for one of these positive qualities during a prayer as Valerie did can be a real blessing to him or her.

5. *Countering the negative.* When a negative thought comes into your mind, or a past hurt he or she caused, an effective antidote is to pray a biblical prayer right in that moment, even if it's just, "Lord, let your favor and blessing shine on my spouse today." Check the "Topical Prayers for Your Marriage and Mate" at the end of the book; choose one to counter the negative thoughts in the weeks ahead, and write it here:

Your Own Marriage Prayer

Based on the verse, 1 Thessalonians 5:18, write a prayer of thankfulness to the Lord for your marriage, for your spouse and what he's done in your life together. Before you write your petitions—what you want God to do in your own marriage and heart—ask for a spirit of gratefulness to infuse your relational and spiritual life. It's a prayer he loves to answer:

Glimpses of God: A God Who Loves Gratitude

R. A. Torrey, the great British evangelist, said that the two words we often overlook in approaching prayer are the "with thanksgiving" part of Philippians 4:6–7[3]: "Do not be anxious about anything, but in everything, by prayer and petition, *with thanksgiving,* present your requests to God. And the peace of God, which transcends all understanding, will guard your hearts and your minds in Christ Jesus" (NIV, emphasis mine).

How often we forget to thank God for blessings he's already given us when we come to ask him for something new! We're like the nine lepers who didn't take time to go back and thank Jesus for their miraculous healing, since they were so busy trucking on down the road (see Luke 17:17).

Just as a spirit of humility draws us to God, thanksgiving is a key to power in prayer. It also helps our faith grow—whether we are praying for our marriage, our children, or a friend. Thanking God for what he's already done or what he's already blessed us with draws us into the very heart of God because he loves a grateful heart.[4] Throughout the whole Bible are examples that show entering his gates with thanksgiving is the way we are to come to God. Here are a few of them to meditate on and incorporate into your prayer life. As you read them, let me encourage you to thank God as specifically as you can for the many gifts he's given you:

- "Oh, give thanks to the Lord, for He is good; / for his loving-kindness is everlasting" (1 Chronicles 16:34 NASB).

- "Be joyful always; pray continually; give thanks in all circumstances, for this is God's will for you in Christ Jesus" (1 Thessalonians 5:16–18 NIV).

- "Let us come before him with thanksgiving. / Let us sing him psalms of praise" (Psalm 95:2 NLT).

- "It is good to give thanks to the LORD, / to sing praises to the Most High. / It is good to proclaim your unfailing love in the morning, / your faithfulness in the evening" (Psalm 92:1–2 NLT).

A Future and a Hope

Chapter Three

"For I know the plans I have for you," declares the Lord, "plans to prosper you and not to harm you, plans to give you hope and a future. Then you will call upon me and come and pray to me, and I will listen to you."

JEREMIAH 29:11–12

Mike heard his parents-in-law's deep Mississippi accents call his name over and over as they tried to arouse him from the deep sleep of anesthesia. It was his second major surgery in three months for diverticulitis. With monitors beeping, tubes coming out of his body, and an IV dripping into his arm, he struggled to open his eyes, until finally he could make out the solemn expressions on their faces looking down on him in his hospital bed. On the opposite side of the bed was his wife Debbie's surgeon.

Confused and bewildered, Mike thought, *What's going on here? How's Debbie doing?*

His forty-six year old wife was in the next room, having been admitted to the hospital three days before for pneumonia that wouldn't seem to clear up despite several rounds of antibiotics. "Nothing serious . . . we just sent off a little of the fluid outside your wife's lungs. Very routine," the doctor had assured him.

But the surgeon's grave expression seemed to communicate a vastly different message. "I'm sorry, Mr. Curry. Your wife has cancer."

A cold, sterile, white ceiling stared back at Mike from behind the faces of Debbie's parents.

"No! No!" he pleaded, barely able to speak. "Has anyone told the kids?"

"Bill broke the news to them," Debbie's mom told him.

"How are they taking it?" Mike asked, tears beginning to pour down his face.

"They're handling it the best they can, just like we are. You rest now, Mike," his parents-in-law said as they left the room.

This couldn't be true. It must be a nightmare or hallucination because of the anesthetic, Mike thought as he cried himself to sleep alone.

Only two months before he had accepted a new assignment as senior pastor of a South Texas city church. When he and his wife, Debbie, and their three kids came to town, they were in great health. But it hadn't lasted long.

From that day in the hospital and for the next eighteen months, Mike watched his wife of twenty-six years die—one agonizing breath at a time—from a rare form of cancer.

Through those long days and months, the grief at seeing the ravages of that deadly disease on the wife he adored tore Mike apart. Just getting out of bed in the morning took all the fortitude he had. Miserable and with little hope for the future, he'd prefer God just take him when his wife died. They'd been together for more than a quarter of a century, and some days he didn't know how he'd go on without her . . .

***

Mike stood at the graveside, the pain in his heart so deep this man—so verbal he could dazzle a whole congregation with a sermon—couldn't muster a word. He felt like he'd just buried half of himself in the ground.

As he and the family left the cemetery, his married son, Jeff, told him, "Dad, you just need to find a nice Christian woman and get married again. You're not a single swinger. You're a family man—and you're only forty-eight!"

"I'll never remarry," Mike replied adamantly. *Never take a chance of marrying another wife who might die before me,* he thought. *Never go through this kind of pain again. I'll just take care of my kids and stay single.*

Within a few months of his wife's death, he resigned his pastorate at the Waco church and accepted a position ministering to single adults in a large Oklahoma City church. Even with a change of city and assignment, as the months dragged on, Mike had very little enthusiasm about life and what was ahead for him. As someone once said, "Where you used to be, there is a hole in the world, which I find myself constantly walking around in the day time and falling in at night." No wonder night after night he slept fitfully and woke up exhausted.

One day in early December Mike rolled over in the guest-room bed where he slept every night (he couldn't bear to sleep alone in the bed he and his wife had shared for twenty-seven years). That morning—for the first time in months—he realized he felt refreshed after a good night's sleep.

Sunlight shone in through the miniblinds onto the red bedspread. As his eyes opened, the thought crossed his mind, *It's good to be alive.*

How strange. That thought hadn't occurred to him in the almost two years since his wife's cancer was diagnosed. He was surprised by the next thought: *Just like Jeff said, I've got to find myself a nice, attractive, godly woman.*

The same man who less than a year before had said he'd *never* remarry felt a desire from the core of his heart. "I need a wife, God. You know I'm not a single swinger. I'm a family man and need a companion. I need a wife."

"We cannot pray fervently without faith and hope. If we approach a door expecting that no one will be at home, or fearing that whoever is at home will receive us coldly, we may not be inclined to knock more than once. On the other hand, the fact that we may have been received with frequent kindness will give us the faith and hope to knock hard a second time. And in the same way, faith and hope in God bring prayer alive and make it persistent."

John White, Daring to Draw Near

But instead of listing the attributes he wanted in a mate, Mike's petition was entirely different: "Lead me to the woman who *needs me the most*. And cause me to fall madly in love with her and cause her to fall madly in love with me."

Working with single adults over the years, he'd heard lots of prayers of single men and women who were longing for a mate. But this kind of petition was different—it was asking for God to choose while he just showed up for service.

Almost immediately a lineup of women he knew came into his mind's eye. All godly women, attractive women, but he felt nothing special for any of them.

He went down the line, by name, talking about each woman with God.

"Okay, this first one is a widow. Is she the one?"

"The second woman—oh, she is gorgeous, inside and out. She's been divorced twice and both husbands were unfaithful to her. Am I going to help mend her broken heart?"

"Now this next woman has never been married before. Lord, am I her dream husband?"

"This fourth one—maybe she's the one, Father. She's going to the mission field soon. Debbie and I served in Africa for four years so I've got experience that might help. Do you want me to go back to the mission field with this woman?"

Moving down the list of potential mates, he eventually got to the last one: a widow named Cyndi who attended his church. He didn't even see her, but her three children were clear in his mind's eye. "Do you want me to be a stepfather to those Lamb kids, Lord?"

Just a few weeks before a friend had suggested he go out with this woman, who'd also lost her spouse. But Mike wasn't interested in her. "Don't you ever mention her name again. She has those kids, two dogs, a big house, and I don't want any part of a big yard and house and blended family. You couldn't even pay me enough money to go out with her."

***

A few miles away, Cyndi was having lunch with her friend Kathy.

"Did you know Mike Curry's moved to town?" Kathy asked her. "I hear they've hired him to join the staff at church. Don't you know him?

"Yes, we went to the same high school camp, sang in a district singing group, went to the same college, and I knew his sister. I guess you could say I know him—but it was a long time ago."

"Didn't he lose his wife? You two might be a good match."

"I'm not interested!" Cyndi said. "I married wild and crazy the first time. I don't think I'll ever remarry, and I'm okay with that. If God drops someone in my lap, then so be it. But he better be the strong, silent type this time. And Mike Curry is anything but silent."

"I still think you ought to consider him. You could have a future together," Kathy said.

The word *future* always triggered memories for Cyndi of her encounter with God on the stairs of Mercy Hospital weeks after her husband Steve's car accident. On his way to teach children's church, Steve had been hit head-on by a teenage drunk driver, causing a massive brain injury.

Seven weeks after the accident, she gave birth to their daughter Kaitlyn in the same hospital where her husband lay in a coma. Only a few days after delivery, she'd been back to keep vigil at the hospital every day.

It had been one crisis after another—spiking fever, staph infection, the possibility of going back to ICU. She felt lower than she'd ever been.

"The longer Steve goes without responding, the less hope he has of recovery," the doctors had told her on their rounds. "Even if he came out of the coma, he'll likely be a quadriplegic."

Waves of sadness and hopelessness engulfed her. *How am I going to take care of my three kids and brain-injured husband?*

As she'd walked down the steps that day, Jeremiah 29:11 came into her thoughts: "I have a future and a hope for you."

"You have to be kidding, God. You expect me to believe this under these circumstances. My husband's in a coma. I have three children,

one a new baby. I don't know how I'm going to physically or finan-
cially take care of them, for starters. And you think I'm going to
believe that your plans for me are good and that I can have hope in
a bright future?"

In that moment she felt like God said, "It's for times like these
that my promise is there. Anyone can believe it when things are
going well. But if it was true before the accident, it's true now."

> "God does not leave us comfortless, but
> we have to be in dire need of comfort to
> know the truth of his promise. It is in time
> of calamity . . . in days and nights of sorrow
> and trouble that the presence, the suf-
> ficiency, and the sympathy of God grow
> very sure and very wonderful. Then we
> find out that the grace of God is sufficient
> for all our needs, for every problem, and
> for every difficulty, for every broken heart,
> and for every human sorrow."
> *Peter Marshall*

"But no one would see these horrible circumstances and believe
this." Looking at what her life was like and her husband lying co-
matose in a hospital bed for weeks on end, she just couldn't get her
mind around that kind of hope.

"Then you can't look at your circumstances. You've got to focus
on me and what I say I'll do in my Word."

It was almost as if God had dared her to have hope and take him
at his word.

Though her mind was fighting all the way, as she opened her car door, she threw caution to the wind and said, "I'll do it, Lord. None of this makes any sense. I see nothing in the situation to give me reason to believe you have a future and hope for me and my family. But because I really do believe your Word is true, despite how things look—I'm going to believe you."

It wasn't easy to keep believing. Sometimes in the hard days and nights that followed, she'd think, *God, Steve was a creative, godly, vibrant father. What a waste of a life. It makes no sense. What's going to happen to us? I don't see how I'm going to go on.* But God kept providing and giving her strength when she needed it—through five and a half grueling years of her husband's hospitalization and rehab, followed by his death from leukemia three days before they were to move into their wheelchair-accessible house.

Now, she'd come to terms with widowhood, worked through the grieving process, and kept her plate full being a single mom of two teenage boys and a daughter. She wasn't looking for a man—especially not one like Mike Curry.

***

Two weeks after the prayer, "Lord, lead me to the woman who needs me the most," Mike had an appointment to meet "the Widow Lamb," as he called her, at the Java Joint. He had asked her one Sunday after church how her kids had dealt with the loss of their dad and how she'd helped them through it. He was worried about how his children were coping after their mom's death. Since she was two years down the road from where he was, could they meet and talk about helping kids cope with grief? Since there weren't any other people their age who'd had the same experience, she agreed.

The rich smell of freshly brewed coffee filled the small restaurant as Mike and Cyndi found a table in front of a brightly colored cold drink machine.

But instead of having a serious talk about grief issues as planned, Mike began to drink in every moment and every word Cyndi said. Both were caught off guard as stardust seemed to sprinkle all over their table—and it was only two in the afternoon. As crazy as it sounded, he wondered, *Is that "Some Enchanted Evening" I hear playing in the background or just a tune going through my head?*

Mike looked into her clear blue eyes. *This woman is beautiful.* Each time she threw her blonde head back in laughter at one of his jokes or stories, he felt drawn closer to her.

And those dangling Santa Claus earrings she was wearing. He'd loved dangling earrings on a woman since he was a little boy.

Suddenly he heard God say, "What are you looking for, Mike Curry, if it's not *her*?" It was true. Cyndi was not only a great person and godly mother who had stood by her husband, Steve, through the ordeal after his tragic accident and death. She was also a fascinating woman he couldn't take his eyes off of.

In less than twenty minutes, Mike fell madly in love.

***

That afternoon, Cyndi called her friend and said, "Kathy, something has changed. I don't understand it, but I'm giddy as a girl in junior high. I can't think of anything but Mike Curry."

Because they were busy with their own schedules, church activities, and children's school events for the entire month of December, they didn't have their first date until the thirtieth. But over one hundred hours of phone conversations helped them get to know each other in the interim.

When Cyndi said, "How is this happening so soon?" over dinner when they finally got together in person, Mike answered, "It's not hard to understand; it's the answer to my prayer."

Mike had asked God for the woman who needed him the most. What he never dreamed was that God was also choosing the woman Mike needed most for *him*.

***

In June the couple—Cyndi in her tailored pink suit, Mike in a handsome black suit—stood before 2,200 people in their church's Sunday morning service, with all six of their children standing on the stairs leading up to the bride and groom. Big video screens showed pictures of the bride and groom in high school church camp when they'd first met, frames of their individual engagements, weddings, and births of their babies. Frames of Cyndi and Mike together during their engagement. In the last scene, they walked across a stone bridge, Cyndi and Mike in the middle, all of their children holding hands.

"Make us thy mountaineers,
We would not linger on the lower slope,
Fill us afresh with hope,
O God of hope." *Amy Carmichael*

When the choir sang "Faithful" by the Brooklyn Tabernacle Choir, there wasn't a dry eye in the congregation. I know, because I was there, and it was one of the most moving weddings I've ever attended. The very people who had prayed earnestly with Mike's parents-in-law and for Debbie through her battle with cancer and who had supported and prayed for Steve, Cyndi, and their children through the last five years of his life and two years of widowhood were witnessing an amazing thing: God's faithfulness in healing two broken hearts and blending two families together.

Of course, although Mike and Cyndi knew without a shadow of a doubt that it was God's plan to cause them to fall madly in love and give them a future as husband and wife, the process of blending their families—with three children each—was a lot more challenging than they ever imagined. They did not breeze through the transitions like a thirty-minute episode on *The Brady Bunch*.

Even though they didn't have to deal with custody issues or children bouncing back and forth between households in a second marriage after divorce, they faced real struggles and conflicts. They came with different parenting and family styles, one highly structured and one more laid back and flexible. There were different expectations and the challenges of building a relationship with a teenage son who wasn't thrilled about having a stepfather and grown kids who took time to get to know their new stepmother.

Though it hasn't been smooth sailing—are any of our lives?—through patience in stressful times and working on issues with a counselor when they hit rough patches, Mike and Cyndi know they are both such better people because of being married. The spiritual growth alone in each of their lives has been worth it.

Cyndi lights up his life, and he's a great gift to her. And after all, she might still be the Widow Lamb if Mike hadn't come along.

God didn't only give Cyndi hope. Her book *Keeping Your Kids Afloat When You Feel Like You're Sinking*[1] has given hundreds of women hope and practical help when they face the loss of their spouse or tragedy in the family. And they both minister to young people in their community and church and have inspired people around the country through a message of hope in God's goodness even in the face of tragedy and loss.

Only four years away from being empty-nesters when their youngest daughter goes to college, Cyndi and Mike look forward to years of enjoying each other and continuing to grandparent the next generation as God brings each new life into their family.

He has given them a future and a hope, and they can't wait to see what else he has in store.

Heart to Heart:

QUESTIONS FOR REFLECTION, DISCUSSION, AND JOURNALING

1. *What's your focus?* If Cyndi had kept her eyes on the overwhelming circumstances of her life, she would have not been able to keep her kids afloat—much less maintain her own sanity. But in her encounter with God on the steps of Mercy Hospital, he reminded her of his truth and challenged her to believe that he *did* have a future and hope for her though she couldn't see it. When she got her focus on God and believed against all odds that he'd do just what he said in Jeremiah 29:11—she experienced an out-of-this-world kind of peace and trust that sustained her in the worst of times.

In the challenging or difficult circumstances of your life, what do you focus on?

2. What was God saying to you as you read this story?

3. *Are your prayers servant prayers or selfish prayers?* If you're single, it's tempting to let your desire and search for a mate become the focus of your life instead of God and what he wants for your life. If you're married, it's easy to pray prayers focused on your own needs and desires.

When Mike prayed, "Let me fall madly in love with the woman who needs me the most," he was in essence praying in a more God-centered, servant way instead of praying a self-absorbed prayer. In the process, God—the gracious Giver—did more than he could have asked or thought in giving him a wife like Cyndi whom *he* needed as much as she and her kids needed him. What kinds of prayers do you tend to pray?

4. "When we move to the place in our spiritual walk that we are God-centered rather than self-centered, then we become like huge cisterns ready to be filled with the peace and joy God created us to enjoy," said counselor Abel Ortega in his new book *Declarations: Transforming Your Pain into Peace.*[2] This week pray and live in a God-centered way and write what you experience:

5. What favorite verses remind you who God is and who he wants to be in your life?

Your Own Marriage Prayer

What is the area of your life in which you most need to be assured that God has a radiant future for you and your family? Based on the key scripture for this chapter, Jeremiah 29:11, write a prayer for your marriage:

Glimpses of God: The God of All Hope

Hope means comfort, expectation, confidence, and trust. Hope is our anchor because it energizes us and gives us the ability to hold on to God in the midst of difficult times. Hope is the music of our soul; it propels us forward when everything looks insurmountable. And just as Cyndi and Mike did, you can experience hope in trials and suffering because of the truth that God is the God of all hope, and Christ in you is the hope of glory (see Colossians 1:27). As you read these verses, meditate on the truth that God's very nature, being a God of hope, can fill you with hope no matter what you're facing:

• "We exult in hope of the glory of God. And not only this, but we also exult in our tribulations, knowing that tribulation brings about perseverance; and perseverance, proven character; and proven character, hope; and hope does not disappoint, because the love of God has been poured out within our hearts through the Holy Spirit who was given to us" (Romans 5:2b–5 NASB).

• "Now may the God of hope fill you with all joy and peace in believing, that you may abound in hope by the power of the Holy Spirit" (Romans 15:13 NASB).

• "This hope we have as an anchor of the soul, a hope both sure and steadfast" (Hebrews 6:19 NASB).

How have you experienced the God of all hope in your life so far? Where do you need hope today?

A Second Chance

Chapter Four

*Now it is time to forgive him and comfort him.
Otherwise he may become so discouraged that he
won't be able to recover. Now show him that you
still love him. I wrote to you as I did to find out
how far you would go in obeying me. When you
forgive this man, I forgive him, too. And when
I forgive him (for whatever is to be forgiven), I do
so with Christ's authority for your benefit, so that
Satan will not outsmart us. For we are very
familiar with his evil schemes.*

2 CORINTHIANS 2:7–11 NLT

Juggling suitcase, purse, and notebooks, Jan trudged in the front door of her home after a week of speaking at five different Christian Women's Club luncheons in cities around the state. Her husband, Jack, was away on business. Their teenage son was still at school, so the house was empty.

Dropping her bags on the bench in the foyer, Jan headed for the kitchen. She brewed a pot of green tea and sipped from her favorite china cup, part of a set of dishes Jack had given her on their last anniversary.

Barney, their beagle mix, peeked through the flap of the doggie door, nudging her leg for much-needed attention. As she stroked the animal's black-and-white coat, she breathed deeply and felt her whole body relax. It had been a hectic week of presenting messages and meeting new people, driving to the next event, and sleeping in guest rooms. In a few days she'd have to prepare and pack again for a weekend conference where she was ministering. It was good to be home.

Looking out the window, Jan gazed at the vivid pink tulips that had sprung up in her garden in her absence. How grateful I am for the life God has given us, she thought. *Almost thirty years of marriage to the love of my life. Three children, eight grandchildren and one more on the way. A church family and a ministry sharing the gospel with women in places I would have never imagined.*

"Lord, you are so good," Jan whispered, her thoughts drifting to the ladies she'd met in the past few days, the young woman who'd accepted Christ for the first time, the plans for her and Jack to meet their family later in the month at their lake house.

The ring of the doorbell interrupted her thoughts. Her brother, Tom, ushered their mother in the door. Since she was in town for a few days, he'd brought her over for a visit.

At the kitchen table Jan served them scones and tea, while her mother caught her up on the report from a recent doctor's visit.

Just then the phone rang. Jan went to the living room to catch it.

"This is Michael Epperson. Did you know your husband has been away on a trip to a Hilton Head resort with his assistant, *who happens to be my wife?*" The man's voice escalated with every word until he was yelling.

"What gave you this idea?" Jan asked.

"My wife just came home and told me about the whole trip," the enraged husband said, continuing to rant about the affair.

"You must be mistaken," Jan interrupted. "Jack has been at a business conference in Raleigh-Durham, North Carolina. He called me after the final session last night and is due home by dinnertime. There's no way he could be with Jennifer. She's at the office."

Even as she protested, a heaviness and dread began to form in the pit of Jan's stomach.

"He may have called you, but he is *not* where you think he is. He's been in a hotel room with my wife. They've been together all week. You must be in serious denial, Jan," he said.

When she tried to ask him a question, he blurted, "Just ask your husband when he gets back where he's *really* been" and slammed the phone down.

Jan dropped her head into her hands as tears of betrayal slipped down her face. Her heart began to race uncontrollably. *What should I do?* Emotions, thoughts, questions she didn't want to face flooded into her mind. *But this can't be true. He must be crazy. Not my Jack. Not after twenty-eight years of marriage. We've raised three children. We've taught Sunday school together for years, spoken for an international Christian ministry. We've been happy. This couldn't happen to us. He wouldn't do this.*

Then suspicions broke through. *Maybe that's why he was so glad for me to go on this trip alone. But no, Jack would never be unfaithful.*

How could she go back in and join the kitchen conversation? She couldn't tell her mom. Not after the death of her son and husband. *She's loved Jack like a son. This would break her heart.*

"I've got to go down to the laundry room and get a load of clothes," she called, heading down the stairs to the basement. On the extra phone line, she called her brother and asked him to come down. He immediately joined her by the dryer and knew something was up when he saw his sister's face.

"What's wrong? What's happened?"

Through her tears, Jan told him about the phone call she'd just received.

"Have you ever done anything like this, Tom?" she finally asked.

"Yes, I was unfaithful once several years ago," he said, dropping his head. "But Carolyn never knew about it. I think she would have left me if she'd found out. I regret it terribly."

"Take Mom home with you. I don't want her to know anything about this. And I need to be alone and figure out what I'm going to do."

Reluctant to leave, he gave her a huge hug. "You know I'm here for you."

"You'd better go or she'll be down here and see me all upset."

Climbing the stairs, he called, "Mom, we've got to get going. I've got a few places to go before I take you out for dinner!"

For the next few hours, Jan went through a whole box of Kleenex. Crying alternated with shock and denial. *I wonder if he'll ever hold me again. I wonder why he's turned to another woman. Will I ever feel his arms around me? Oh, what can I do, Lord? What can I do?*

"God works powerfully, but for the most part gently and gradually." *John Newton*

She wanted to crawl into her bed and stay there. But their teenager would be home from baseball practice soon, ravenous for dinner.

At six p.m. Jan heard the key in the front door. When Jack appeared in the kitchen, she said, "We've got to go somewhere and talk. I've fixed food for Jonathan but I've lost my appetite."

They drove to a local café. Over cups of coffee, Jan said, "Jennifer's husband called me today very upset and angry. He told me you and his wife had spent the week together. Is it true?"

Jack's face registered shock and dismay that Jen would tell her husband about their relationship and the trip. "I shouldn't have done it. I'm so sorry, honey. And it's no big deal. I'll stop seeing her. I promise. I didn't want to hurt you or the kids."

Not a big deal? Maybe not to him, but nothing her husband said that night soothed her wounded heart. All her "why's" in the days to follow were met with excuses, apologies, promises. Crying herself to sleep that night, she wondered if he could keep them or if she could ever trust him again.

Four days later, Jan's friends picked her up for the two-hour drive to the women's conference where she was doing a session on the power of prayer. Jack came out to the car to help her with her book bag and suitcase and to say good-bye. Before she got into the car she told him, "I don't know how I can possibly do this."

"You always said you could do all things through Christ," he said before walking back in the house.

On the drive to the conference center, Jan was beside herself. *If my friends knew what was going on in my life, they'd be shocked. I wish I'd stayed at home. I shouldn't even be speaking today. I have nothing to say. How could this be happening to us? This is unreal.*

She couldn't tell her friends what had happened. They had happy marriages and none of them had ever been through anything like this. Jan sat in silence and inner turmoil for the entire trip.

They joined three hundred other women in the auditorium for the first session, and Sharon Whiting, the speaker, came to the podium. When Sharon announced that her message was entitled "The God of Second Chances," it got Jan's attention. She told a story about her best friend, a godly woman who had served God in speaking and writing for several years. But when she went to a counselor for some personal problems, it wasn't long before she went from crying on the man's shoulder to sleeping in his bed, and ended up leaving her marriage and getting a divorce.

Her friend had come to see Sharon for advice, and they went for a long walk. "I've committed adultery. Could God ever use me again?"

Sharon told her friend that over and over in the Bible God sought out the lost ones, that He could restore what the locusts have eaten. He was the God of second chances.

Jan didn't hear anything else the speaker said. Her mind wrapped around those four words that gave her hope that maybe her marriage wasn't over. *Lord, I'd love to go talk to Sharon. She said she'd be by the pool during the break if anyone wanted to talk to her. . . .*

But there were so many women lined up during the break to talk to the speaker that Jan didn't try. Besides, as the area rep, she had to get her notes together for her luncheon message, which was next.

"Jan," the emcee of the luncheon called to her when she entered the dining room. "Did you know you're at the head table? There's your seat." When she went up on the platform and sat down, Jan noticed the place card next to her. Sharon, the speaker, had already been placed there.

Though she'd never met this woman, during the luncheon Jan began to pour out her story about her husband's affair. She couldn't tell her friends yet, but somehow this woman who she'd never met but who believed in a God who gave second chances seemed a safe place. After listening to her, Sharon gave her the name of a Christian counselor and a Christian attorney.

Getting up to the podium after salads and desserts had been eaten and whisked away took every ounce of courage Jan could muster. Her hands shook with nervousness but grace carried her through the message.

When she returned home, she looked up the name of the counselor and began meeting. One of the important things the woman advised her was to pray, "Lord, help me to see my husband through your eyes, to love him as you love him, and to value him as you value him."

"The love of God is great and strong; yes, we can speak of an ocean of love. That love gives us the strength to forgive and even to love our enemies. That love is a source of power and victory during the most terrible crises of our life, but also in everyday life." *Corrie ten Boom*

"You have all the rights and privileges of the wife. Use them often," the counselor added. Jan did, but her heart was broken. She knew about his girlfriend. She knew they were keeping in touch and often he came in very late. When Jan and Jack were invited by friends to go out for dinner, they went, but it was like a charade. They both knew things were not right.

At the same time, Jan continued to get calls and nasty notes from the enraged husband, as if it was *her* fault his wife had left him.

Her husband stayed in the home because they were in the middle of planning for two family weddings for their daughter and a son.

But after the last wedding in December he came one day to get his clothes and a lamp and some of their furnishings. He had already been transferred to a different office one hour away and was moving into an apartment there.

The aloneness and finality she felt after their separation was almost overwhelming. The only thing that kept her going was knowing that even though her husband had left her, God hadn't forsaken her. The evidence of his care was too present. He provided her with many friends, with great prayer support and loving family. With her brother Tom, who was always there when something broke or she needed moral support. With her sons and daughter, who constantly encouraged her even while puzzled and disappointed with their father's choices. With a volunteer job at the local hospital as a buyer in the gift shop that helped fill the time. With Abby, a friend whose husband had divorced her and remarried another woman. Abby came over anytime Jan needed her and they often went out to dinner together.

One of her lifelines was a Christian attorney who was more interested in restoring a family than making a lot of money from a nasty divorce. When Jan arrived after a one-hour drive to his office for her appointments, instead of asking her to list her husband's indiscretions or strategizing how to nail him, the two of them got down on their knees and prayed for the marriage. The attorney never sent her a bill. He did suggest she keep a journal and record any compliments or gifts from her husband, or any time they made love. Since he'd already moved out, Jan didn't have much faith in the possibility of any of those things, but she promised to write everything down.

Early on, God gave her 2 Corinthians 2:7–11, which says:

> Now it is time to forgive him and comfort him. Other-
> wise he may become so discouraged that he won't
> be able to recover. Now show him that you still love
> him. I wrote to you as I did to find out how far you
> would go in obeying me. When you forgive this man,
> I forgive him, too. And when I forgive him (for what-
> ever is to be forgiven), I do so with Christ's authority
> for your benefit, so that Satan will not outsmart us.
> For we are very familiar with his evil schemes.

When she hurt to the core, she remembered the prayer her counselor suggested she pray. Through her tears she asked, "Lord, help
me to see Jack as you see him, love him as you love him, and value
you him as you value him."

She prayed it often, month after month, though her husband's
infidelity and abandonment for another woman cut to the core of
her being. "Lord, help me love Jack as you love him."

Slowly but surely, through the months and years of praying for
her husband and for the grace to love him as God loved him and to
see him as God saw him, forgiveness came. She was forced to think
How does God see Jack? instead of being consumed by anger. God
gave her his perspective to see Jack as a person who had worth and
value even if he'd made bad choices. As a man who had lost his way.
She sensed that sin had gotten in the way and he'd gotten caught
up in it. At times she even saw he still had some feelings toward her,
like when he asked to spend the night or spend time with her. She

realized he felt trapped in the relationship with his assistant and couldn't get out. He felt so responsible that the girlfriend had left her husband and divorced him for Jack, and that she had younger children.

As she prayed, "God, help me to love him with your love," he reminded her how he loved Jack and had died for him. Although she was dying on the inside, as those petitions went heavenward, her love for her husband increased and bitterness had no chance to get lodged in her soul. As she drew close to God and leaned on him, she saw things differently and found new hope even in the lack of change in her situation, with no sign of restoration or return.

"When you forgive you in no way change the past—but you sure do change the future." *Bernard Meltzer*

When she was served with separation papers, her lawyer advised her to answer with her journal entries. The opposing attorney told his client if he wanted a divorce, he'd better stay away from Jan.

When her life was in turmoil, she struggled with whether she should stop ministering, so she asked God. One night the enemy attacked as she was on a four-day speaking trip. She'd never asked for decisions or signs, but that night she prayed he would show her the next day if it was in his will for her to continue sharing the gospel and her testimony at Christian women's clubs. The very next day there were seventeen decisions for Christ, the most they'd seen in one meeting in years. She knew he was saying, *Keep on.*

As the second and third year passed, Jan went through a season of thinking she couldn't possibly go on.

"God, I can hardly stand this; it's hurting me so much," she said one morning.

Suddenly he gave her a word picture she hadn't seen or thought of in years. A woman sat down to do some writing and saw a little cocoon outside her window. Each day she looked at that cocoon and still nothing had emerged. Impatient, the woman decided to cut the cocoon a wee little bit. Something came out, but it wasn't what she expected. It was the shriveled body of the butterfly, whose wings were so weak and underdeveloped, it couldn't flap them. In an hour the little creature died.

God broke through that metaphor to say, "I know it's dark and lonely, but trust me. It's not time yet."

Hearing those few words from God helped her persevere.

One night she couldn't sleep and dialed the number for the local time and temperature, which also included a daily homily. "You can face the future with confidence," the voice said. "It's three a.m. and the temperature is 41 degrees."

"Lord, help me to see Jack as you see him, love him as you love him, and value him as you value him," she prayed in the dark.

One of her darkest moments came when she'd taken her last son to college and come home to an empty house. In a few weeks, she had to have surgery. Although Jack was at the hospital during the operation, when she was discharged, she had to drive herself home. She curled up on the bed they'd shared for so long and wept and wept. After that, she felt she should let go and let him have the divorce.

The next time Jack came by the house, she said, "Just get a divorce if that's going to make you happy."

Tears ran down his face.

"I'm going to go over there and tell her it's all over," he said. But he couldn't do it. Before long, the divorce was final.

As far as Jan knew, their life together as a couple was over.

But that holiday season on Christmas morning, she heard a knock at the door and Jack walked in, his face all red from the bitter cold. He'd walked four miles to get there when his car wouldn't start, because he wanted to be with the family.

A few hours later when it was time to go, he asked, "Would you drive me home?"

Jan agreed.

"How is it you'd do this for me after all I've done to hurt you?" he asked as Jan drove him back to his girlfriend's apartment.

"Because I care about you and love you enough to not want you to freeze to death."

***

Six years after the day she first learned of her husband's affair, Jan and Jack stood before family and friends in their home to be reunited in marriage. Joining them were Jan's counselor and four couples who'd been there all along. Their children and their spouses. Jan's attorney, who had quit his law practice to go into marriage counseling.

The minister that remarried them was a former realtor. He had come to know God through his wife, whom Jan had taken to a Christian Women's Club where her life was changed. Her husband became a Christian and eventually quit his job and attended seminary to become a minister.

"When I was in the real estate business," the minister said, "I used to go into a home and wonder what story the house could tell. Well, this house could tell quite a story. They always say anyone objecting to this marriage should speak up. I'm going to ask anyone who is in *favor* of this wedding to speak up please.

"I want to be the first to speak," Jack said. "I turned my back on God and my family, but they never turned their backs on me. When I left home, none of you left me out of your prayers. I want to thank you all. I have asked my God for forgiveness, my dear wife for forgiveness, and my children for forgiveness. They have all forgiven me.

"I thank God that I'm getting a second chance today to marry the girl I love."

"I told Mom to get on with her life," their daughter said. "How thankful I am that she never listened to me!"

A son expressed his happiness for their remarriage and for answered prayer.

Jan spoke last and said, "I have the opportunity to marry the man I have always loved."

Heart to Heart:

QUESTIONS FOR REFLECTION, DISCUSSION, AND JOURNALING

1. *A powerful prayer.* You may not be dealing with the unfaithfulness of your spouse, but the prayer she prayed—"Lord, help me to see him as you see him, to value him as you value him, and to love him as you love him"—is a profound and valuable one for any of us. How could it make a difference in you and your spouse's lives and destiny?

2. *See him as you see him.* We all have times when our perspective on our mate gets clouded by our own issues (the "me, myself, and I" syndrome) or hurt, disappointment, or misunderstanding. In those times we need our hearts unlocked. I've found it's very eye opening to pray, "Help me to see my spouse as you see him." When I do so in my own life, God usually shows me something new. He gives me a fresh appreciation for Holmes's creativity or generosity; he gives me compassion when Holmes is in a stressful situation.

Let's look at the first part of the prayer: "Help me to see him as you see him, Lord." How do you see your mate right now? What things stand out when you think about him or her?

3. As you begin to daily pray this prayer, use this space to record any new perspectives you gain about your husband or wife:

4. *Love as you love him.* As I explained in chapter 1, when we are out of love, at the end of our ropes, and without warm fuzzy feelings for our mates, God still loves him or her with an everlasting, unconditional love. He died for our spouses. For the next thirty days, pray, "Lord, help me to love _____ as you love him (or her)" and record what happens within (in your heart) and without (in your marriage):

5. *Value him as you value him.* Dr. Emerson Eggerichs, in his book *Love and Respect*, said that while women's greatest need is for their husbands, by words and actions, to show their love, men most need something else. Citing Ephesians 5:33, "Each one of you also must love his wife as he loves himself, and the wife must respect her husband," he said that men desperately need their wives to show they have value by how they treat them—in other words, by respecting them.[1] Jan's prayer for God's help in valuing her husband as God valued him (even though he'd made some seriously bad choices) eventually contributed to the restoration and healing of their marriage. How could you apply this prayer to your own marriage?

6. *Patient endurance.* When we're in the depth of a conflict or hard situation, and it's the hardest thing to endure, we can't imagine a good outcome. We become weary of praying for relief. Sometimes we protect ourselves by closing the door to the relationship and arranging some other happiness on our own. Our society certainly supports this way—give up, throw in the towel, and find somebody better. What are the prayers you're tired of praying? What do Psalm 37:34 and Hebrews 12:3 say to you?

Your Own Marriage Prayer

If you are living a difficult marriage or have experienced major rejection or smaller hurts like being shut out emotionally, instead of looking for the nearest exit you can turn to God. He can and will give you the inner strength and wisdom to make wise choices and give you his love for your spouse when yours is seriously damaged. He can also fill you with forgiveness that may lead to reconciliation and a second chance. Using 2 Corinthian 2:7–11 as a foundation, write your prayer for your marriage.

Glimpses of God: The God of Second Chances

One of the things that gave Jan hope in what she went through—from early on and throughout the painful period of separation and divorce—was knowing God was a God of second chances. How many of us need a second (or third or fourth) chance in an area in which we mess up or make poor choices—in our job, in marriage, in parenting?

Read how each of these people in the Bible were restored by God and given a second chance in which the Lord's purposes were fulfilled:

- After Moses killed an Egyptian (see Exodus 2–4)
- After David's great sin with Bathsheba (see 2 Samuel 11–12)
- After Peter denied Christ (see Matthew 26:31–75)
- After Peter and Barnabas disagree and part ways (see Acts 15:36–41)
- After Hezekiah became ill (see Isaiah 38)

Just as God gave these Bible people second chances because of his grace and mercy—and just as throughout history, many people such as St. Augustine, John Newton, Chuck Colson, and Franklin Graham, to name a few, received a second chance—he offers a fresh chance to you and your spouse. The key factor is repentance, turning away from your own way and to God. But be encouraged—there is no pit so deep or dark his grace can't reach you! When we come with a contrite heart, the Lord will be faithful to restore and redeem our mistakes.

In All Our Ways

Chapter Five

*Trust in the Lord with all your heart
and lean not on your own understanding;
in all your ways acknowledge him,
and he will make your paths straight.*

Proverbs 3:5–6

It was a mild December night, and Mi Tierra Restaurant in San Antonio's Market Square shone more brightly than usual. An extra layer of Christmas decorations added to the glitter of lights and tinsel left up year round. The noise of talking and laughter and the music of strolling mariachis set a festive tone as Greg and Martha ended their day spent shopping in jewelry stores.

Over plates of spicy cheese enchiladas and guacamole, the engaged couple was almost giddy over finding the perfect rings. Talk turned to invitation lists and family members who might be expected to attend the wedding from out of town.

"Vicki might bring the twins," Greg said. "And Dorothy and Mike will probably bring Gina and Deana, and Grant and Deborah will probably come with their twins."

"Wow. How many sets of twins does your family have?" Martha asked.

At the same moment, their eyes met and grew wide with a kind of shock.

"I never really thought about it, but twins do run in my family," Greg said.

Feeling like her stomach had dropped to her knees, Martha choked out, "You mean we could have twins?" Though she'd taught a classroom of students, the thought of handling multiples of babies in her own home filled her with anxiety.

"Yeah, I guess so."

Sitting quietly for a moment as the idea soaked in, they touched hands across the table.

"You know," Martha said, "Although that sounds a little overwhelming to me, I know whatever kids God gives us—even if they come in multiples—he'll give us the grace and provision for them!"

Agreeing on that, they turned their attention to their enchiladas.

Greg and Martha's romance hadn't begun in the typical college boy-meets-girl, boy-dates-girl manner. They got to know each other over a number of years as they worked side by side in the youth ministry at a church. Each had grown up in a Christian family. But Greg had come to his own renewal with Christ in early college and Martha in her late twenties.

From teaching and counseling teens and their parents, they'd seen what they *didn't* want their family life to be like: parents who showed up all smiles and hallelujahs at church, but then threw keg parties for their teens; dads who taught Sunday school but failed to honor their own marriage vows. They'd seen this result in confused, insecure kids with parents whose dynamic ministries claimed all their time and attention and left their kids on the sidelines eventually resenting the very God their parents served. They didn't want their family to operate like that.

The more they talked, the more they began to know each other's heart, so that when they did fall in love and Greg asked Martha to marry him, they began to take those principles and see how they would apply them in their own home. They wanted to be intentional about marriage and parenting, not just leave everything to the shifting winds of culture and busy lives.

"Emotional peace and calm come after
doing God's will and not before."
Erwin W. Lutzer

They decided any children God gave them would be their first mission, and that whatever ministry they took part in would be done as a family, including each member. The families they did want to emulate invested daily in each child's personal spiritual health. Martha and Greg purposed for the best of their time, prayer, creativity, and interaction in guiding their children into personal relationships with Jesus because that was what they believed was most important.

Also, imprinted on Martha's memory were the two verses in Isaiah (55:12 and 54:13) God had given her promising that if she would trust him and his ways, he'd give her a home filled with joy and peace, and that peace would be a hallmark of her kids' lives.

As she shared those promises with Greg one night shortly after the engagement, he asked, "What would our home need for that to be true?" Pushing the wedding plans and lists aside, they began to share their thoughts and dream before God of the family they hoped to establish.

***

On a Saturday a number of months later, Greg followed his fiancé around department stores, trying to be enthusiastic as she held up silverware, glasses, china, and skillets. Later, the couple lounged at an outdoor table, drinking coffee and splitting a piece of cheese-cake.

Martha looked up from checking off wedding errands and asked, "Greg, Pastor wants to know if there is any special Bible verses that we want him to use in the ceremony. What do you think?"

"Those verses from Isaiah that you were talking about would make a good benediction. It would be great to have those promises spoken over us as we leave," Greg responded. "But what about the major verses read at the beginning of the wedding?"

As the night sky faded from turquoise to purple to black and stars joined the reflection of colored lights on the San Antonio River, talk drifted from which pottery pattern they should choose and whether they would entertain more formally or informally to what the spiritual atmosphere of their home might be.

Martha leaned forward and lowered her voice. "I've dreamed of a home where trusting God and following in his ways was the first thought and focus."

Greg leaned toward her. "What would it be like if we'd already es-tablished that in every decision, and it wasn't a question of 'Will we or won't we follow God?' but just 'What would God have us do?'"

"Trustfulness is based on confidence in God, whose ways I do not understand. If I did, there would be no need for trust."
Oswald Chambers

Martha's eyes shone.

"I don't want us to live situation to situation," Greg said. "I really want the foundation of our home to be trusting God and following his Word—in how we treat each other, our finances, our childrear-ing, every aspect of our life as a family."

"And we'll immediately seek him for decisions," she added.

"*That's the verse*—Proverbs 3:5–6. It's what we'll use in our wed-ding but also bank our life together on: to trust in the Lord with all our hearts and not rely on our own understanding," Greg para-phrased. "In everything we do, we'll acknowledge him, and then we can trust that he'll be faithful to direct our paths."

"It's a great prayer for our marriage," Martha agreed. "And I really liked the blue and white dishes best, didn't you?"

***

It's been a long time between that blissful day picking housewares to the twenty-nine years they've experienced together. Although Martha and Greg's lives since saying "I do" in 1978 has held the same bumps and jolts that all people face—ten grueling years of caring for Martha's mother who suffered with Alzheimer's, the ill-ness and deaths of all but one of their parents, times of financial hardship, and trials and challenges that are part of life on earth—they've experienced a deep core of peace and joy at the center of their marriage, in the *midst* of their trials. They've been able to handle the external stress with a minimum of strife or stress in the relationship. Not because they're better or more special than other families, but because of God's grace and their belief in the promise that if they trusted him, he would direct them in all parts of their life together. The audio (what they said) and the video (what they did) matched, and this made an enduring impact on their own chil-dren and the teens they worked with over the years.

They agreed that if God's Word and his way are clear, then that's what we'll do. When they came to a place when perhaps the choices weren't so clear, their prayer was always, "Direct our path, Lord." When life-changing decisions needed to be made, they kept living by that verse they'd prayed during their early years together: "God, help us to trust you with all our hearts and not lean on our own understanding."

One of those hard decisions was where to put their two children in school—whether to place them in the San Antonio public schools or the Christian school their church operated or to homeschool them, which as an English teacher, Martha could handle well. Many friends were starting to homeschool and urged them to do the same. "We've got a great homeschool support group you could join! Your kids won't face the temptations of public schools! They'll be in a protected environment," they said.

Others urged them to put Annie and Matt in the Christian school. "They'll get a better education; it's safer, and you could teach in the English department, Martha. We could use your skills there!"

But as they prayed—instead of leaning on their own understanding of what looked good to them or their friends—God showed them very clearly he'd called them to the public schools. And not just the kids, but Martha and Greg themselves.

You see, not only had these two striven throughout the years to follow God in everything, but they had daily worked to model that same faith to their children. Because of this, the family as a whole was committed to lifting their schools to God. Every year before school started, the whole family went to the campuses each of them would attend that year (including the high school Mom taught in) and do a Jericho March—a prayer walk around the perimeter of the campus. They prayed for students and families, administrators, and teachers, and that each of them would make a positive impact on those they learned from and worked with. They continued this practice throughout the two children's elementary, junior, and senior high years, and in this way Martha and Greg continued to live their faith and model their marriage prayer of Proverbs 3:5–6.

There were bumps along the way, of course. For instance, when Matt got to his freshman year of high school, it was anything but a Christian environment to put your kid in. This was a rough inner-city school with gangs, drugs, and fights as common occurrences. Only a few other students showed up for See You at the Pole and FCA (Fellowship of Christian Athletes) had one other member. But during their years of interacting with the school, the fruit of their obedience was the salvation and transformation of countless teens' lives who were influenced by Matt, their daughter, and themselves.

However, the biggest challenge to their faith is something they are still walking through as a result of what happened on a Sunday in 2005. On that day Kyle, a dear family friend and son Matt's mentor, was electrocuted while baptizing a student.

Greg and Martha stood there, stunned, as Kyle's life was tragically ended before their and the whole congregation's eyes. During the remainder of that day, they comforted grieving young people, while their son was assigned the daunting task of fielding questions from the media as word of Kyle's death spread across the country.

"Relying on God has to begin all over again
every day as if nothing had yet
been done." *C. S. Lewis*

In the months that followed, Martha and Greg have continued to process their own grief at seeing someone they admired, respected, and loved die in a sudden, traumatic way. The immediate questions and their emotions were nearly overwhelming. "Why, God? This is not right! This is not fair! So many are hurt so deeply. You could have saved him. God, how could you?"

They had no answers on that day, and they have no answers still. What words could they say? None seemed adequate. What could they do when they are crushed themselves, yet know they have to minister to their son and many others looking to them?

But they remember those words, treasured and proven over and over: "Trust in the Lord. Lean not to your own understanding."

It is still a process this family is walking through. Simply, to trust. He is God, and he is good.

They trust him, and he still directs their paths.

Heart to Heart:

QUESTIONS FOR REFLECTION, DISCUSSION, AND JOURNALING

1. *Where do you trust God?* Early on in Martha and Greg's relationship, they decided to trust God with their marriage, their future children, finances, careers, everything. They realized God is concerned about our *whole* life, not just that he cares in a compartmentalized way about the church part. God wants to give you guidance and care in every part of your life too.

This is truly a very intentional couple and you may be thinking, *God only provides this kind of support for people like them.* But the truth is the Lord offers his guidance and peace to whosoever will come to him, depend on him, and ask. What parts of your life have you entrusted to God in the past?

2. Where do you trust God and allow him to direct you now?

3. Where do you not trust God? What areas of life—money, job, children, relationships, etc.—do you have a harder time opening up to God's guidance and therefore handle things yourself rather than invite his active help?

4. The two verses from Isaiah—55:12 and 54:13—referred to in this story are also terrific verses to pray for your marriage and life. How would you personalize them to pray over your own family and children?

5. *Peace in the midst of things.* Though Martha and Greg's family experienced trials and stress as any other family would, the hallmark of their home throughout the years of marriage has been peace. Not because they are a "special" couple or are better than others, but because God keeps his promises. They knew they could bank on his promise—that if they trusted in him with all their hearts and in all areas of their lives, he would guide their steps and give them peace. God is a God who keeps his promises. So you can proclaim, "God, you said this and I'm going to live believing that it's true and you never lie." What is a promise of God you can believe and live by today?

Your Own Marriage Prayer

Although this couple made Proverbs 3:5–6 their prayer for their marriage and family when they were young, it is *never* too late to turn to God to trust him with all your heart. Your internal compass can be God's Word instead of feelings or culture's opinions. Instead of leaning on your way of doing things, you can invite him to guide and direct you. Based on this verse, write a prayer to God for your life and family—bringing to him the things you want to trust him with.

Glimpses of God: A God of Peace

The word used for *Lord* in Proverbs 3:5–6 is a covenant name meaning "a God we know and who knows us." We can trust people only if we know them. The same goes for God. And although God reveals himself through the Old Testament (see Psalm 119:165, Psalm 37:37, Proverbs 3:17, and Psalm 4:6–8) we know him with even greater revelation through Jesus. Isaiah 9:6 tells us Jesus will be called "Wonderful Counselor, Mighty God, Eternal Father, Prince of Peace" (NASB). Jesus said, "Peace I leave you; my peace I give you" (John 14:27). And Romans 15:33 says, "The God of Peace be with you."

The Lord doesn't promise us a trouble-free life, however. In fact, he let us know ahead of time that there will be problems and tribulations in this world for all of us, but that he has overcome the world and will be with us: "I've told you all this so *that trusting me, you will be unshakable and assured, deeply at peace.* In this godless world you will continue to experience difficulties. But take heart! I've conquered the world" (John 16:33 MESSAGE, emphasis mine).

Do you believe in God's promise? This promise—a deep abiding peace no matter what happens—isn't only for a couple like Martha and Greg but for all those who trust God with their whole heart. Make the choice to consciously trust God each and every day. If so, no matter what this world brings, you can rest in the knowledge he is with you.

Twice Adopted

Chapter Six

Long ago before he laid down earth's foundations, he had us in mind, had settled on us as the focus of his love, to be made whole and holy by his love. Long, long ago he decided to adopt us into his family through Jesus Christ. (What pleasure he took in planning this!) He wanted us to enter into the celebration of his lavish gift-giving by the hand of his beloved Son.

EPHESIANS 1:4–8 MESSAGE

The lyrics of "Blessed Be Your Name" poured out of the radio as Michael and Allison headed for lunch on their way home from church. From the first time they'd heard it, soon after the miscarriage of their son, Owen, it was as if God had penned the words directly onto their hearts: *Blessed be your name on the road marked with suffering, though there's pain in the offering.*

Although it was still difficult to see any blessing coming out of their loss, they still believed that God was calling them to have a family.

"Do you think it means anything?" Michael asked, pulling into Wendy's for lunch. "The song, I mean. Do you think God's trying to get our attention?"

The restaurant was filled with the usual after-church crowd. Grabbing a table by the window, Michael and Allison slid into seats directly beneath a poster for the Dave Thomas Foundation for Adoption.

They had talked about adoption, even before they had married six years earlier. With so many children needing homes, they had always planned to adopt—but not until they had their own biological kids.

"If it wasn't the song, that poster would certainly get my attention," said Allison, nodding toward the window. "It doesn't seem like a coincidence. Maybe we're supposed to be doing more than just talking about adoption."

Tired of messing around on this one, and having experienced three heartbreaking miscarriages, the couple *really* wanted to figure out what God wanted them to do and *do* it. So they decided to set aside a week for fasting and praying—asking God, "Do you want us to adopt or to keep working toward biological children?" Believing he was the one who'd given them the desire to have children, they wanted to find out how he was going to accomplish that in their lives.

After a week of seeking God, they sat on the couch together in the living room and asked each other, "What do you think God's will is for us? What's he put on your heart?"

The answer surprised them both. "I'm getting a no," Allison said, "I don't think we're supposed to adopt."

"I feel the same way," said Michael. "It's as if at this point, with all of the miscarriages we've been through, adoption would be taking the easy way out. I feel like I'm wanting to adopt right now because our pregnancy track record is awful and I don't want to watch you go through that again. I don't want to go through it all again."

"Neither do I," she said, as memories flooded in her mind of the morning she'd come home from the hospital following the loss of their baby. Four weeks on bed rest and on all kinds of medication had left her exhausted and sick. Worse still, she'd left the hospital with empty arms, wondering *Why is this happening again? Doesn't God want us to have a child?*

"I just keep thinking about the verses that talk about there being no fear in love and that perfect love casts out fear," Allison sighed. "The truth is I'm afraid to get pregnant again. I know we've been through all the medical stuff and there's nothing wrong with either of us, but how many times does God expect us to volunteer for heartache?"

"Still, if we're both getting a no on the adoption, then it looks like God's pointing us back to biological children and that means getting pregnant again," said Michael.

"The greatest experience, the one which shakes a soul with hopes and fears, the results of which are never ending, and incidentally, the only one which pays the biggest dividends, is to be found in the adoption of children." *Anonymous*

Inching forward in faith, 1 John 4:18 became the prayer of their heart: "Perfect love casts out fear, because fear involves punishment, and the one who fears is not perfected in love" (NASB). Yet even as they prayed together to overcome their fear, to fully place their trust in the Lord to give them a child, the thread of adoption continued to weave its way into their lives. Several months later, Michael and Allison found themselves at a concert where the miracle of adoption was the artist's personal testimony. The pull on their heart was too strong to deny.

"Has God changed his mind?" Allison asked on the drive home. "Or have we changed our hearts?"

"I think it's a bit of both," Michael answered. "We've shown our willingness to face our fears and pursue God's love by being open to another pregnancy. Maybe now that our hearts aren't ruled by fear, we're ready to show the kind of love that we always thought adoption would be. I mean, when we first talked about it years ago, we wanted to adopt because God adopted us into his family, and I think that hasn't really changed. It's still mirroring the heart of God by sharing the gospel in a practical way, by loving someone else the way that Christ loved us."

Once the fear was gone, the doors of their hearts swung wide open to adopting a baby. They told everyone they knew they wanted to adopt, researched different processes, and decided to pursue an open adoption through a national agency.

Over the summer, a friend named Jackie from church approached them about a friend of hers who was pregnant and considering adoption. "I've told her all about you and that you want to adopt. I think she might be interested in meeting you," she said.

"We're working with an agency, so she would need to contact them," Michael and Allison told Jackie.

The idea of adopting Susan's baby terrified them. There were a million reasons not to get involved: Susan lived in town, just a twenty-minute drive. She used to attend their church. They knew too many of the same people. It was just too weird. It certainly wasn't the scenario they'd imagined.

"Send her to this agency," Allison said, scribbling down the web site for Jackie. "They'll give her lots of support and help her find a lovely family for the baby."

A few months passed while, Michael and Allison prayed for the future birthmother of their baby.

"Lord, you already know who she is, even if we don't. While we're waiting to meet her, please keep her and the baby safe. Bring people into their lives to encourage her. Help her find our agency and show her that there are people ready and willing to love and help her. Help us get ready to meet her. To share our lives with her. To share God's love with her."

They realized that for something as wonderful as adopting a child to happen in their lives, someone else would have to experience a great loss. And they knew from losing a child of their own how terribly difficult that would be. They had no idea if their birth mom would be older or younger, healthy or ill, in a safe relationship or a difficult one. But almost every day they came together to lift her up in prayer.

Jackie continued to mention Susan, but they still weren't interested. Too close, too strange, too uncomfortable.

Not too long after, a pastor connected them with a young woman in another state looking for a family for her unborn son. After several phone calls, Michael and Allison flew to meet her, almost sure that she would ask them to be the adoptive parents of her child. With only four weeks before the due date, excitement started to build.

Maybe this is the one, Allison thought as she stood in an empty nursery. *At last, the Lord is going to give us the desire of our heart.*

But God had other plans for that young life and the mother chose another family. They didn't see it coming or understand why. Their meeting had gone so well. They had so much in common. "Why are you closing this door?" they asked, back on their knees before the Lord.

Trust me, God whispered to their weary hearts. *Trust me with all of your heart even if it doesn't make sense to you.*

Moving forward with their agency, Michael and Allison finalized their home study and put together a letter for the agency to send to prospective birthmothers.

"Hello! We believe that adoption is an amazing way to create a family," it read. "Now that we are ready to take that step, we are committed to an open adoption that showers a child with your love and ours. You must have a lot of questions about your child's future family. We hope that this snapshot of our lives opens a door to the answers . . ."

In December of 2005 their letter went into circulation. And then there was nothing to do but wait. Wait and pray. But as in many cases when God places us in the waiting room, He was working out a miracle just beyond our gaze.

"[Adoption] carries the added dimension
of connection not only to your own tribe
but beyond, widening the scope of what
constitutes love, ties, and family. It is a
larger embrace." *Isabella Rossellini*

Unbeknownst to Michael and Allison, one of Allison's coworkers was also a friend of Susan's and had shared their story with her. "If you are serious about giving this child in love through adoption," she told Susan, "you will never find a better family for him than with Michael and Allison."

In the interim, the expectant mother had contacted the agency, been screened, and had signed all the forms. Two months before her due date, she was given hundreds of letters from waiting families who matched the profile of qualities she wanted in an adoptive family.

Flipping through the letters, she found Michael and Allison's. They seemed so familiar, but why? She wanted a Christian family, but there were lots of letters from Christian families waiting to adopt. What made these two people different?

Then it hit her. The smiling couple gazing up at her from the pictures below was the very same couple Jackie and Patty had talked about. She knew she needed to meet them.

"You'll never guess who just called," Allison said to Michael one day soon after as she grinned into the phone.

"Who?" Michael asked.

"Susan. And we're having dinner with her next week. Can you believe it?"

Neither of them could. At several points after their first birthmother had chosen another family, Michael and Allison had talked about Susan. But the idea always seemed too complicated. Too close. Too difficult.

"You and I both know we keep closing the door because it's not easy," said Michael one night, "not because we know for sure that's what God wants. I don't think that we've even really asked him about this."

Allison agreed. "If our original desire to adopt was to mirror God's love for us by welcoming a child into our family and showing his birthmother the love of Jesus, then Susan certainly fits that description."

"I guess it's back to praying," sighed Michael.

It *wasn't* easy. How do you pray for something that you don't really want?

"God, if adopting Susan's baby is your plan, it's certainly not what we planned. But if this is your plan, change our hearts to match." They figured if this was his will, he'd *definitely* have to work on their hearts to bring them in line with his heart.

They met Susan for dinner at a local Thai restaurant and began the tentative journey of getting to know each other. The meal was much more comfortable then they had anticipated, full of laughter and talk about their childhoods, even talk about the future. Still, questions remained. How would a future relationship work when Susan lived so close?

Allison mulled the question over and over in her mind. *Everything seems right Lord, but I don't know if I can do this.* There are just too many people involved, too many people who know us both. She imagined bringing the baby to church or to the grocery store. Would people say, "Oh, this must be Susan's baby"? *Will we ever be viewed as his parents by people who know us both?*

Working through her daily Bible study notes, Allison opened her Bible one morning to Genesis 22. God had opened Genesis to her in a new way as she walked with Abraham and Sarah through their desire for a child and God's plan for fulfilling his promise.

In that day's reading, God had asked Abraham to sacrifice his great gift. A paragraph from her study notes leapt from the page:

> Even in the midst of personal agony, only the person who gives all to obey God's clear command experiences unspeakable joy and radiant expectancy (hope because of unshakeable faith in God's character of tender love and utter faithfulness to His own loved

child) . . . To be preoccupied with imaginary situations usually results in being blind to God's present
call to obedience along clearly defined paths."

"How could I have been so stupid?" She laughed, calling to Michael in the next room as joy welled up inside of her.

"This isn't Susan's baby and he isn't our baby. He's God's baby
and God already has a plan for his life." The worry, the fear, the
hesitation to love Susan and the baby lifted. In its place, God's perfect peace filled her soul. She knew at that moment that God was
going to choose them for this baby.

"Time and experience has taught me a
priceless lesson: any child you take for
your own becomes your own if you give
yourself to that child." *Dale Evans*

The next evening they met with Susan again. It was like a meeting of old friends. *She's done so much to take care of this child,* Allison
thought, gazing at the woman across from her. Any questions about
Susan's past or her choices melted in the light of the love they all
three had for the child she was carrying.

As they were walking out to their cars, Susan stopped and said,
"You know, at the end of our first dinner I went home and slept
deeper and more peacefully than I had during the entire pregnancy.
This just feels right for you to be my baby's parents."

Bursting with joy, Allison grabbed Susan in a hug. "Oh wow.
Thank you!" What else can you say?

Pulling out of the parking lot, Michael and Allison starting calling their families. "She picked us!" they shrieked into their cell phones. "We're having a baby!"

With only six weeks until Susan's due date, they swung into full-time baby frenzy: preparing the nursery, sorting through the mountains of hand-me-down baby clothes their friends had given them, and finalizing their hospital plan and future contact arrangements with Susan.

Working out the logistics of the hospital stay, future contact, and how the open adoption would work was complicated and challenging. The relationship between birthmother and adopting parents is delicate, like a spider's web. Handcrafted and beautiful, but fragile to the point that too much pull in either direction can destroy it all. Sometimes, the process demanded so much faith that Allison was ready to cut their losses and leave. But God's grace was sufficient, his presence obvious, and his compassion perfect.

Liam Patrick Shaw made his arrival on March 22, 2006, and came home to live with his family on March 24. From the tip of his nose to the points of his toes, his parents love him with all their hearts. They plan to love and nurture him into a relationship with Jesus Christ, which would make him twice adopted—once into their family and forever into God's family.

As they look into his beautiful face, they know Liam is God's child, placed in their arms for his growing up years. He has blue eyes like his mother and his father's sense of humor, and when he laughs, Michael and Allison know that's God's plan is perfect.

Heart to Heart:

QUESTIONS FOR REFLECTION, DISCUSSION, AND JOURNALING

1. *Seeking God's plan.* Throughout their journey, Michael and Allison learned how important it is for us to invite and obey God's plan and guidance—rather than our own agendas—in every area of our lives. And that even when our plans go awry and we can't see his hand, to trust his heart and know he has a better plan. He told us: "For my thoughts are not your thoughts, / neither are your ways my ways" (Isaiah 55:8).

Is there some area of your life in which you have relied on your own thoughts and agenda instead of finding out what God's thoughts and direction may be concerning the issue? If so, why?

2. *Getting on board.* When Susan chose Michael and Allison the day after God changed Allison's heart, it was as if he was just *waiting* for them to get on board with his plan before he could bless them with the desire of their hearts: their son Liam. In what ways have you resisted God's way or plan because it didn't match up to yours?

3. Struggle can strengthen a marriage—if we allow prayer to connect our hearts with God's heart so he can be the glue that binds us

together. Although it was challenging, working through their grief and frustration by praying together brought Michael and Allison to a deeper level of intimacy and a deeper relationship with each other and God. In what way is a current struggle in your life strengthening your marriage?

4. *Responding to God's promptings.* How do you think he wants you to respond in this situation?

5. *Adopted by God.* Allison and Michael desired to adopt because they believed that adoption is the ideal picture of what God has done for each of us in making us his children through Christ. What are your impressions of God? Is it difficult or easy for you to relate to God as his beloved, adopted child (not an orphan or stepchild)? If so, why?

Your Own Marriage Prayer

Many couples who experience loss and grief move away from each other and have a hard time connecting—thus putting more stress on the relationship and creating higher divorce rates for these couples. Instead, as you write your prayer in the following space, let me encourage you to ask for the insight and ability to reach toward each other in prayer as you deal with problems and difficulties instead of letting the problem tear you apart.

Glimpses of God:
Abba Father, Our Heavenly Papa

Because God is our adopted Father, he encourages us to behave like his very own children, adopted into his family—calling him "Abba, Daddy," (see Romans 8:15–16). And as Larry Crabb said, "Unless we become as little children who approach our heavenly Papa just to be near Him, something in our hearts will keep us confused and frustrated when we ask God for what we want."[2] God encourages us to come to him for the purpose of being near him and knowing him, not just getting something.

As you read the verses below, consider how this view of God as your heavenly Daddy would impact your prayer life:

• "Long ago before he laid down earth's foundations, he had us in mind, had settled on us as the focus of his love, to be made whole and holy by his love. Long, long ago he decided to adopt us into his family through Jesus Christ. (What pleasure he took in planning this!) He wanted us to enter into the celebration of his lavish gift-giving by the hand of his beloved Son" (Ephesians 1:4b–8 MSG).

• "See how very much our heavenly Father loves us, for he allows us to be called his children, and we really are! . . . Yes, dear friends, we are already God's children, and we can't even imagine what we will be like when Christ returns. But we do know that when he comes we will be like him, for we will see him as he really is" (1 John 3:1–2 NLT).

• "Whoever humbles himself like this child is the greatest in the kingdom of heaven. And whoever welcomes a little child like this in my name welcomes me." (Matthew 18:4–5)

As you go through your busy life today, let me encourage you to reflect on these truths, to thank God for the reality that you (and your spouse) are his own children, and to receive the grace he wants to lavish upon you (see Ephesians 1:7–8a).

Make Us One

Chapter Seven

*The goal is . . . to become one heart and mind—
just as you, Father, are in me and I in you, so
they might be one heart and mind with us.*
JOHN 17:21B MESSAGE

When Katie and Vance got engaged, it didn't take long to discover how different they were in almost every way. In her job as a university professor, she was forever in meetings, teaching classes, and dealing with instructors in the department she chaired. All day, however, Vance sat alone in his office speaking into a recorder and pouring over financial plans and proposals. At the end of the workday, he was ready to go out and be with people. But after the constant conversations with students in and out of her office and the noise stimulus, Katie had something entirely different in mind: sitting with her fiancée in a quiet room with a glowing fire and a good book.

They were polar opposites in other ways. His home life had been like the movie *Pleasantville*: no harsh words, conflict, or show of emotion was allowed, whether positive or negative. Katie's family's emotional life was more colorful, open and communicative. Vance was an early riser. Katie was a night person. She was a creative, big-picture thinker, and he was a detail-oriented, sequential-thinking guy. In a group situation, he was more gregarious and knew how to work the crowd. She was quieter in a big-group setting and cultivated deeper but fewer friendships.

However, the greatest differences showed up in their spiritual life—especially every time Sunday rolled around.

Lost in praise, Katie's hands were raised as she sang with all her heart in the morning worship service at the Baptist church. Beside her, Vance stood there looking bored. Tight-lipped, with arms folded across his chest, he looked relieved when the service was over. His preference was to go to the Episcopal church, where he could kneel at the prayer rails and read the confessions, petitions, and thanksgivings from the Book of Common Prayer with the congregation. Nothing spontaneous or enthusiastic. Quiet, formal, and reverent—that was how he liked church.

When Katie joined him at his church, everything seemed to her like a formula. The words out of the prayer book seemed archaic, leaving her cold and feeling far away from God's presence. But when she looked over at her husband, she could tell he was deeply moved.

Before they married, they'd agreed they would go to church but didn't hammer out the details of how and where they'd do that. She had no idea the way they'd operate would be to go to different churches.

Growing up, her mom (and her dad when he wasn't working the night shift) escorted their three girls—occasionally in darling identical dresses Mom had made—to church. For Katie, church wasn't just a spiritual lifeline but a relationship base as well, something her family joined in together.

To Vance, church was a singular experience between him and God—not a social or community experience. And he saw nothing weird about being a member of a different church than his wife.

After all, that's exactly what his parents had done and it worked just fine for seventy-two years of marriage.

"You see roses; he sees thorns. You see God vacuuming the sky; he sees God dumping the vacuum bag. You're planning the next party, and he's worrying about all the trash the party will make; in fact, he worries about all the trash in the whole world, plus the shortage of water, the national debt, and any number of other serious matters." *Barbara Johnson*

From their earliest days together, his parents were members of different denominations. Mom was a staunch Christian Scientist and Dad a Methodist, and "nary the twain shall meet," as the old saying goes. They liked keeping their spiritual lives independent of each other, and had no intention of changing to join the other.

So Vance was raised going one week to Sunday school with the Christian Scientists and the following Sunday attending church with the Methodists. His parents were loving and devoted—but even into their nineties, they still didn't attend church together. So it was just fine for him and Katie to forever switch between the Baptists and the Episcopalians—that was all he knew.

To make matters worse, Katie *loved* to talk about God and her faith. To Vance, faith was a private matter. When he brought up a problem going on at his company, Katie would say, "Let's go ahead and pray aloud together now," but he'd sigh deeply, get that strained, uncomfortable look and tell her to go ahead and pray. When she was finished, he added the "Amen." The only aloud prayers he'd ever made were from the prayer book with the rest of the church members.

When Katie shared what God had spoken to her in morning prayer time, he had two responses: either "Oh, really?" or "You had a conversation with God today?" Then when what God showed her came to pass, he felt intimidated by his super-spiritual wife—and clammed up even more.

Through the years, her heart's cry continued to be that from John 17:21: "Father, make us one." She asked the Lord over and over that somehow, someway, he would make her and her husband one heart and mind about one church where they would be united as a family and share their spiritual life at home. After they had children, that longing for spiritual unity grew.

When they moved to a suburb with their little girls, she found an interdenominational church nearby (thinking maybe they could compromise) that she eventually joined. Vance went to the early Episcopal service and occasionally came with his wife and their two daughters to her church. But he let his wife know with his lack of participation that praise and worship just wasn't for him. He still gave his tithe to the Episcopalians, and since she rarely went to his church, the spiritual distance between them grew. Week after week, she saw other couples enjoying church together and longed for that in her marriage.

Things finally came to a head after six years.

One Sunday she looked over at her husband down the pew on the other side of their girls and realized he was just gritting his teeth,

bored as ever. With all her hoping and praying, he was no more enthusiastic about her church than their early days of marriage.

He is holding up his end of our pre-nup agreement by showing up, she
thought, *but I'm not. What I'd hoped to gain just by being together in
church just isn't there for us.*

She finally decided that even though she didn't enjoy the Episcopal church, it was time for *her* to change, to hold up her part of
the bargain and get their family where they could attend church
together.

As hard as it was, that next Monday morning Katie turned in her
resignation at her church.

"I just want us all together worshiping at the same church. This
isn't working," she told Vance that night at dinner. "Let's go be Episcopalians. I'm not going back to my church. The girls and I are
joining yours."

To her surprise, he called her best friend, Theresa, and said,
"Come over here. Katie's lost her mind! She's leaving the church!"

The very next Sunday he went out and joined his wife's church.
Finally they were all united in one place. Or were they? Vance still
wasn't moved by the service. He liked some of the couple friends
they had developed over the seven years they were there, but as
time went on, it was obvious he was still just showing up on Sunday
morning for his wife.

"A happy marriage is the union of two
good forgivers." *Robert Quillen*

Two years later, Katie suffered a bad case of pneumonia. After
three rounds of antibiotics, her lungs were not getting better. Her

doctor said he was going to have to admit her to the hospital if something didn't change pretty soon.

The middle of that night, she got up, a cough racking her body every few minutes. With a fever of 103 degrees, she was weak and getting worse—and knew she was desperate for a touch from God.

Instead of waking up her husband or going to the ER, Katie began to worship the Lord, and worshiped nonstop until around four a.m. Suddenly the presence of God seemed to fall so heavily in the room that all she had to do was take a deep breath. As she breathed in, it was like the breath of God filled her, driving out infection and breathing fresh health into her body. In a few moments, her health was restored and later that week, the doctor confirmed it.

In the very same moment she felt God's presence so strongly, she heard him say something she didn't expect: "I'm separating you from your church. I want you to attend Grace Community."

"What, Lord? Surely you must be mistaken. It must be my high fever," she responded. She'd heard of that little church. It didn't even have a real church building, but met in a storefront in the city. She didn't know who the pastor was or what he taught. But the one thing she knew was that she didn't have *any* best friends at that church. The thought of leaving the place and the people she loved upset her so badly she didn't mention it to her husband.

Six weeks later, they were on a rare vacation without the children. On top of a mountain in Colorado early one morning, they sat outside on a deck of their condo drinking coffee and looking at the sun coming up over a spectacular range of mountains.

I've got to tell him what I think God said, Katie thought.

"Honey, it was probably because I had such a high fever or maybe I was hallucinating. But I thought I heard God say that we were to leave our church and join Grace Community. I don't really have any interest in going there—it's small and we probably don't know anybody there—but I just thought I ought to tell you."

He listened quietly until his wife was finished rambling. In the quiet morning, they listened to birds sing and watched lazy clouds drift over the mountain top. Finally, he turned and looked right in her eyes. "I've known for a year God wanted us to do this, but I told him I wouldn't be the one who would tell you. He'd have to."

He took another sip of his coffee and read the newspaper while his wife sat in stunned silence.

When they returned home, she asked Vance, "What do you want to do now?"

"Let's go resign our membership."

That week they met with their pastors and lovingly told them God was moving them to another church.

The next Sunday, as they sat drinking coffee she asked, "Where do you want to go today?" thinking surely he wouldn't say the little storefront church. Maybe he'd like to attend church with one of his parents. They'd be thrilled.

"Let's go visit Grace," he said.

So they did. Halfway through the service, he leaned over and whispered, "None of our best friends are here, but I think this is where we're supposed to be."

"Love is blind, but marriage restores its sight." *Georg Christoph Lichtenberg*

They visited Grace Community for a while, and then one Sunday went to a different church where they knew a lot of people. After the service, when she waved to a group of friends as she got in the car, he said, "Don't even think about it. Let's go back to Grace."

Still, Katie was convinced she wasn't going to make the decision this time around. She wanted her husband to take the initiative and find a place where he could worship God.

They went back and kept visiting regularly. Then one Sunday in November, during a service at Grace, Vance whispered to her, "It's time to join," as he got out a membership card and filled it out.

It began to dawn on her that they weren't joining this church because it offered what her husband liked, what Katie liked, or what their children liked but because it was what God wanted for them. God knew that Vance, a financial analyst, could relate to messages by a pastor who had been a businessman and had a master's degree in finance. As time went on, he grew to respect his pastor and receive his teaching, which helped him grow spiritually. He and Katie both found areas to serve and in time they made plenty of friends. And although he didn't suddenly start enjoying praise music, Vance sang the words and engaged with God and the people. Slowly, mysteriously, they became more and more of one heart and mind with the Lord. Instead of trying to please themselves, their families, or one another, they knew beyond a shadow of a doubt that this was the church God had assigned them to.

And ultimately, that's who they both wanted to please.

However, their different spiritual styles didn't disappear overnight. They didn't become clones of each other or lose their individuality. Katie still likes to talk about her faith; Vance still likes to savor and ponder his quietly. He isn't as demonstrative as his wife, but they pray together at home, and sometimes he enters in as well. She listens for the spiritual discernment God gives her husband, and he's found that the Lord does speak to his wife because she makes it a priority to spend time with him and listen.

After eleven years, this church remains their spiritual home and they have no plans of leaving. As their hearts and spirits blend together, they've both found a contentment and joy in being at the place God planned for them and continue to see his purposes unfold along the way—even when there are bumps in the road.

Heart to Heart:

QUESTIONS FOR REFLECTION, DISCUSSION, AND JOURNALING

1. *After the honeymoon.* After a few months or years of living with our beloved on a day-by-day basis, some of the little differences we once barely noticed or were charmed by start to irritate us. In what ways are you and your spouse different or opposites?

2. Spiritual incompatibility is prevalent in lots of couples. So don't feel alone if you, like Katie and Vance, have different church backgrounds or spiritual differences. You may marry thinking you have a similar belief system and then discover that one is a veteran prayer, and the other less mature in relating to God personally. One likes to pray aloud, the other prefers praying silently. One regularly reads the Bible, the other doesn't pick it up except in church. In what ways do you harmonize spiritually with your mate?

3. In what ways do you clash or lack unity: prayer, church attendance or preference, or other areas of spiritual life?

4. *What are the roadblocks?* Growing in spiritual unity is usually a slow process that takes time, and one step is coming to understand the foundations we grew up with and how they influence aspects of

our marriage and spiritual journey. What were each of your foundational experiences with church? What did your respective parents model to you (praying aloud or silently, having devotions as a family or separately, etc.)? How are they alike and how are they different?

5. *Collision course.* Coming into harmony—and the obstacles to that unity—is different for each couple. What are the current obstacles you see to experiencing oneness as a couple?

6. What do you long for the most? What would be your "wish list" for things you'd love to blend more harmoniously in your spirit-to-spirit connection?

Your Own Marriage Prayer

Maybe you're thinking, *We're so different, how could we really be one, in this or any other area of our marriage?* Wherever you and your mate are now regarding your spiritual life together, let me encourage you that God is able to blend you together like a symphony. Nothing is impossible to him! It may take persevering prayer over a period of time, but he is there for you and it's his idea that you grow in oneness.

Whether you are in harmony with your spouse in the choice of the church you attend or have differences of opinion, styles of worship, or beliefs, we all need to grow spiritually with our mates. Not only in church attendance but in our life together in prayer, in sharing Christ, in passing on a legacy of faith, hope, and love to our children and grandchildren. Write a prayer based on John 17:20–21 that would reflect your greatest desire and God's intentions expressed in this passage for his working in this area of your marriage:

Glimpses of God: A God of Unity

"What is on God's heart is clearly spelled out in Scripture: that husband and wife be one," said Dr. Emerson Eggerichs in his book *Love and Respect.* "I am told that when blue blends with pink, it becomes purple, and that purple is God's color—the color of royalty."[1]

God wants that royalty, that oneness to be reflected in all areas of our life together, for it brings glory to him and joy to us. Psalm 133 says it is wonderful and pleasant when we live together in unity and harmony:

> For harmony is as precious as the fragrant anointing oil
>> that was poured over Aaron's head,
>> that ran down his beard
>> and onto the border of his robe.
> Harmony is as refreshing as the dew from Mount Hermon
>> that falls on the mountains of Zion.
> And the Lord has pronounced his blessing,
>> even life forevermore. (Psalm 133:2–3 NLT)

Just as the oneness of the Father, the Son, and the Holy Spirit are expressed in the Trinity, he desires that we be one. Life, peace, blessing all flow from spiritual unity between husband and wife, brothers and sisters in Christ—not only for them but for future generations.

The Blessing

Chapter Eight

*My lover said to me, "Rise up, my beloved, my fair
one, and come away. For the winter is past, and
the rain is over and gone. The flowers are springing
up, and the time of singing . . . has come."*

Song of Solomon 2:10–12 nlt

Stephanie and her friend Kelly stopped at a kibbutz, a hostel only
yards from the shores of the Sea of Galilee. Kelly, thirty-nine, was
five months pregnant, but traveled with her friend while her husband stayed behind to run the company they owned. This was a
pilgrimage she hoped would prepare her for motherhood.

Stephanie had come to Israel for a different reason: she was
searching desperately for hope.

One night halfway through the journey as the two women lay in
their twin beds, Stephanie confessed how devastated she was that
her divorce was final.

"In a few years I'll be forty," she cried. "All my hopes of being a
wife and mother are gone. Even if by some miracle I met someone
now and fell in love, I'd be too old to have a baby by the time we
got married."

Kelly listened to her friend. Then after a few minutes of silence,
she said, "I think God has something wonderful in store for you,
Steph. His word says 'No eye has seen, no ear has heard, / and no
mind has imagined / what God has prepared / for those who love
him'" [1 Corinthians 2:9 nlt].

Seeing Stephanie's look of doubt, she added, "And that applies to *you*."

"Maybe God has good things in store for other people," Stephanie protested, "but not *me*. I've had two failed marriages, years of mistakes and messed up relationships."

Her mind trailed off to the years from ages eighteen to thirty-five, when she'd "wandered in the desert." Although she'd been close to God in her childhood and teen years, when she went to college, she left God behind. Drinking and dating replaced youth group and Bible studies. Slowly, one bad choice led to worse choices until she didn't recognize herself anymore. After living with her boyfriend her senior year and getting pregnant, she'd gotten an abortion. Then she figured she was cut off from God's blessing of having a baby in the future. She'd engaged in casual sex for fifteen years and had a disastrous first marriage. Loved her second husband, who broke her heart when he ran around and lied to her.

In those years, she related to God like Santa Claus . . . visited him once a year and the rest of the time made a list of what she wanted him to give her. After her first divorce, she prayed for God to send her someone to love, even wrote it on paper and gave it to him in a little wooden prayer box someone had given her. That relationship only lasted fourteen months. One day she cried out to God, "*Why?* Why did you do this to me? I asked you to send me someone I could love," and she heard the voice of God inside her head. He said, "I did."

A few months later, she realized what God meant was that he *had* given her someone she could love who would love her with an everlasting love—and his name was Jesus.

Still, she thought God couldn't bless her. "I don't deserve it. I haven't been good enough," she told her friend Kelly now.

"But that's not the point. You love God *now*, don't you? You've given him your life and are trying to do life his way?" Kelly asked.

"With all my heart. In fact when I ran back to God, I found the man of my dreams, my First Love—the only one who would never let me down."

"Then that's all that matters. He means this promise for *you*, Stephanie."

"Just as I am Thou will receive, will welcome, pardon, cleanse, relieve; because Thy promise I believe." *Charlotte Elliot*

"How can you say that, anyway? How can you be so sure?"

"Because God has given me faith to believe it for you," Kelly answered.

Those words of hope wrapped around Stephanie's heart like a warm quilt when she was too wounded to believe for herself.

The next day as they traveled by bus to Nazareth, Kelly turned to her friend and asked, "Can I pray with you?"

Stephanie felt awkward, but they held hands while Kelly quietly prayed that God would give Stephanie faith to embrace and receive the life he had in store for her, blessing her in ways she couldn't imagine, just like that verse in Corinthians said.

***

Though Kelly's baby son arrived a few months later and she was caught up in the responsibilities of parenthood, the two women stayed close and prayed daily for each other that God would bless their lives. In the years that followed, Stephanie had a few dates, but didn't meet anyone she was interested in. Since she'd given up on both men and marriage and turned to serving God, she experienced a renewal in her personal and spiritual life. She had found her "first love" in Jesus Christ and was no longer looking to a man to fulfill her deepest desires or fill the void inside. And gradually she grew content with a lifestyle of aloneness and loved the opportunities God opened for her as a radio host and newspaper columnist.

Five years after that prayer in Israel, Stephanie met a younger man named Michael. "Only friends," she told her family when they asked about the guy she was spending time with.

When Michael expressed deeper feelings for her, she thought, *He can't be serious about me. I'm thirty-nine and he's only twenty-eight. We're probably only supposed to be friends.*

But their relationship grew and grew until the two fell deeply in love.

With more than thirty-four years of dating experience between them, they decided not to follow the patterns of their past relationships, but to build a partnership God's way. They went to see a friend who was a Christian counselor.

"The ideas I'm suggesting will seem extreme to you," Jim told the couple, "but they are biblically based and they *work*."

He instructed Michael and Stephanie to restrict their time together in the beginning months of their courtship. Keep building their friendship. Then form a spiritual connection that would eventually lead to an emotional connection. They were also to promise to limit physical touch to *only* hugs and kisses—no long romantic

With Stephanie's track record of two failed marriages, and her family history of divorce (her parents when she was six, her grandparents, aunt, great-grandparents), she had a great desire to build a healthy marriage. Instead of the world's version of dating as usual, where the physical relationship is first, here are some things Stephanie and Michael learned about developing a marriage to last a lifetime:

• Avoid spending one-on-one time alone. Too much temptation!

• When having dinner together at one of your homes, invite another couple.

• Build foundations for married life by reading a book for engaged couples together and discussing the questions. For example, write a biblical definition of love after reading 1 Corinthians 13.

• To build spiritual connections, go to church together. Talk about God's interaction in your lives by asking each other weekly, "How have you seen God this week? How has he been working in your life?" Allow God to be the center of your relationship and life. Pray together conversationally, about decisions, needs in your jobs, wedding plans.

• Continue to build a friendship by getting to know each other. One way to encourage dialogue is to fill out an extensive personal inventory full of questions you would never discuss otherwise, such as the grade you liked best in school, a favorite memory growing up, who your teachers were, what you wanted to be growing up, how you each came to know Jesus. Include questions like, "Who am I? Where am I going?" along with practical questions about debt, savings, and financial habits, and share the answers with each other over a period of many weeks.

• Maintain contact through e-mail and talking on the phone, especially if you live far enough away that you can't see each other every day.

These are the things Stephanie and Michael cultivated in their relationship. The results of their efforts? They not only became very good friends but are still best friends after several years of marriage. They also built a healthy emotional and spiritual connection, which led to a beautiful physical connection and close bond of love after they married.

embraces were permitted. And of course it followed that with this approach, sex was postponed until the wedding night.

They followed the plan and built their relationship radically different, even opposite, than they had in prior romances.

It was tough not being physically intimate once they fell in love. Time and time again, their counselor stressed that those who were obedient to God and formed a relationship His way would receive a blessing.

Strangely enough, Jim never specifically mentioned what that blessing would be. It became an inside joke between Michael and Stephanie every time they wanted to go too far or rush their relationship. "Let's wait for that blessing" or "Boy, are we going to be blessed for this!" one of them would say with a look of longing. Yet as hard as it was, as the months of engagement went on, they were obedient to this new way of relating.

On Valentine's Day, at forty years old, Stephanie married the man of her dreams. The wedding Scripture God gave them was from Song of Solomon 2:10–13:

My lover spoke and said to me,
"Arise my darling,
      my beautiful one, and come with me.
See! The winter is past;
      the rains are over and gone.
Flowers appear on the earth;
      the season of singing has come,
      the cooing of doves
      is heard in our land.

The fig tree forms its early fruit;

the blossoming vines spread their fragrance.

Arise, come, my darling,

my beautiful one, come with me."

That passage wasn't only a collection of verses read at the service. It was also Stephanie's prayer of gratefulness to God. The bad things *were* behind her. All the rejection, disappointments, and failures. The new had come.

They spent the following days as honeymooners in every sense—hanging on to each other's words, wrapped in each other's embrace, and craving to spend every spare moment together. One morning in March, the two of them were in the bathroom getting ready for their work days. Michael rubbed shaving cream over his heavy black beard.

"So, what do you think the blessing was that Jim always told us about?" he asked in a serious tone.

She kissed the back of his neck. "What do you mean? Isn't being married to me blessing enough?" The couple did have a marvelous spiritual, emotional, and physical connection with each other and were soul mates despite their age difference.

But Stephanie, too, found herself wondering about the promised blessing from God their counselor had talked about. Was it real or just a ploy he'd used?

"God can heal a broken heart, but he has
to have all the pieces." *Unknown*

Six weeks after they were wed, Michael woke up with his throat tight and inflamed. He'd struggled with strep throat since his teens and knew the symptoms all too well. He made a doctor's appointment. Sure enough, it was strep.

A few mornings later, Stephanie woke up and felt sick, too. Her throat ached a little, but mostly she felt queasy and nauseated.

"Aw, you've got strep." Michael shook his head when she listed her symptoms. "Better go to the doctor. You need antibiotics. It's the only way you'll get well."

Seeing how sick her husband had been, she wanted to get to the doctor and start medication as soon as possible. She managed to get an appointment that day.

Previous visits to this doctor taught her that he always asked the date of her last period. She went to the calendar, flipped to the prior month, and made a mental note of the date. She cocked her head. *That doesn't seem right.* She counted the squares since the last day of her last period.

Stephanie held her breath. She was eight days late.

But it couldn't be possible. At thirty-two her gynecologist had said her chances at getting pregnant declined with each period. And her biological clock had been ticking for a long time after that. Another physician added to those fears by saying that miscarriages and deformities increase with AMA—advanced maternal age.

The couple wasn't actually trying to conceive, but then again, they weren't doing anything to prevent it. *Surely not. Anyway, we just got married a month ago.*

Late that afternoon, she discovered she didn't have strep throat. To Stephanie's amazement, the doctor confirmed with a blood test that she was pregnant. Medical studies and well-meaning friends who'd forewarned the difficulty of her conceiving at forty years old were mistaken.

But what would she tell Michael? They both wanted kids, but so soon?

She pulled into the garage and parked. She remembered her girlfriends describing the cute ways they announced their pregnancy to husbands, friends, or family. One friend got a big cookie at the mall with *Congratulations, Dad* written in icing. Another bought a tool belt and embroidered "Daddy" on it, then filled the pockets with baby powder, pacifiers, baby wipes, and diapers. One even framed an ultrasound picture. But Stephanie was too shocked to be clever.

She walked in the house and found Michael in his closet, sorting dirty laundry.

"Hi, honey," she said, bending to kiss him.

Michael looked annoyed. "Have you seen my black socks?" he growled.

"I don't know. Maybe I washed them. Did you check the laundry room?" *Why are we discussing this? I have something big to say,* she thought.

He continued sifting through the mountain of clothes. "I really need those socks."

She tried changing the subject.

"We need to talk. Come sit on the bed," she suggested.

Michael scooped up a pile of clothes in his arms. "What is it? I don't want to sit down. I need to find my socks."

"I went to the doctor today."

"Do you have strep? Did you get antibiotics?" Michael walked past his wife.

"I really need for you to sit down," she repeated.

"Stephanie, don't play games. What is it? Tell me now!"

"I'm pregnant." It was the first time she'd said those words. A wave of emotion crashed inside and feelings of joy flooded her mind, heart, and soul.

"Right," countered Michael. He walked off to load the washer.

At that moment, Stephanie realized she should have waited and planned something more memorable like her friends had to announce the news.

But in a rush, Michael was back in the bedroom. His face was white. "Are you serious?" he asked. He grabbed Stephanie up in a bear hug, kissing, laughing, and twirling her around.

Nine months later, Stephanie gave birth to their own personal blessing, a healthy, beautiful daughter, Micah Faith, who she never imagined she'd hold in her arms. Named Micah for her father, Michael, and Faith, for the steady belief in Stephanie's future that her friend Kelly had held for her so many years.

Heart to Heart:

QUESTIONS FOR REFLECTION, DISCUSSION, AND JOURNALING

1. How do you picture or perceive God when you are praying, whether for your marriage, your own life, or a friend? Do you see him like Stephanie did in her wilderness years—as a Santa you tell what you want on Christmas Day? Do you see him as an elderly grandfather in a rocking chair in heaven, not able to help us much now, although he did great things in the past like part the Red Sea and save Daniel from the lions? Do you have a picture of a God who disapproves of you and is just waiting to judge you and zap you because of past or present wrongdoing? Or as a ruler of the universe too busy and preoccupied with the Middle East and the affairs of nations to be concerned with your problems?

Or do you see him as Wheaton professor Sam Storms described God, as the "Infinite Giver" whose "heart is filled with joy and delight in us, and he loves nothing more than to shower us with gifts that far exceed our capacity to envision or articulate them."[1]

Write here about how you think of or picture God:

2. *Who God really is.* How you think about God really impacts whether you pray at all, whether you approach prayer as a big obligation or duty, or whether you love to come into God's presence and connect with him.

What would you have to believe about God to pray with faith the way Kelly did?

3. *Snapshots from Scripture.* If your view of God is fuzzy or you have a hard time connecting with him, the best place to discover who he really is is in Scripture. As Larry Crabb said in *The Papa Prayer*, "Don't assume your view of God is correct. Realize your experience with authority figures has shaped your view of God . . . Always check out your impressions of God—and what you've been told—with Scripture."[2]

Knowing God through his Word is a lifelong pursuit; we won't finish until we see him face to face in heaven. But in the Bible he gives us many snapshots of who he is and reveals himself over and over. Here are some places to start. Write beside each verse what you learn about God in the words and phrases:

Isaiah 30:18

1 Corinthians 2:9

Hebrews 1:3

John 14:9

3. *Looking for love.* Sometimes we look to our husbands or wives for the love we desire and need to fill our hearts and make us happy. But as Stephanie found, whether single or married, Jesus is the only one who can be our first love and truly satisfy our souls' longings. We can't depend on our spouses to meet all our needs and bring us joy on a continual basis. That's too big a burden for a human being.

Being mortals, we don't have perfectly unconditional, unfailing, everlasting love. Look up Jeremiah 31:3. What does it tell you about God's love for you?

4. *The time for singing has come.* One of the ways God gave Stephanie back the years she had lost was pairing her with someone younger (which she would have never planned for herself or imagined) and blessing her with a little daughter to keep her youthful as she runs after her in her forties. God chose Stephanie, but he has also chosen you and wants to bless you. He has great things for every one of us who commits his or her life to him and follows him. What are some of the ways God has restored things you thought lost?

5. *Making good choices.* Proverbs says making good choices that are based on God's wisdom rather than the world's ways leads to life

(see Proverbs 4:13, 20–22). Stephanie and Michael made a decision to make good choices—a choice that was radically different from the world's way, or their previous way, of building a romantic relationship. This choice led to life and blessing. In what choices or areas of life has God challenged you to live differently than our culture dictates?

Your Own Marriage Prayer

What is the "winter" in your own life? Where do you need God to bring the beauty and newness of spring back—in your communication, your physical life, your finances, or a relationship? Based on the area of struggle you described in the questions above and the Scripture that begins the chapter, write out your own prayer to God for you and your spouse.

Glimpses of God: A God of Restoration

Stephanie's story is such a beautiful picture of how God restores. He delights in restoring what the locusts have eaten (see Joel 2:25), whether that is through our own mistakes or the damage others have inflicted upon us. He goes after the one sheep out of the ninety-nine that is lost. He is the one who makes everything new (see Revelation 21:5).

Look at the following verses that demonstrate God's promise of restoration, and be encouraged to pray for, believe for, and experience his restoration in your own experience:

- "Your righteousness, O God, reaches to the highest heavens.
    You have done such wonderful things.
    Who can compare with you, O God?
You have allowed me to suffer much hardship,
    but you will restore me to life again
    and lift me up from the depths of the earth.
You will restore me to even greater honor
    and comfort me once again." (Psalm 71:19–21 NLT)
- "Turn me again to you and restore me, for you alone are the LORD my God" (Jeremiah 31:18 NLT).
- "Come, let us return to the LORD. He has torn us . . . now he will heal us. He has injured us; now he will bandage our wounds. In just a short time he will restore us, so we can live in his presence. Oh, that we might know the LORD! Let us press on to know him! Then he will respond to us as surely as the arrival of dawn or the coming of rains in early spring" (Hosea 6:1–3 NLT).

- "He restores my soul" (Psalm 23:3).

Let me encourage you no matter what is going on in your life to spend a few moments in praise to the Lord, for being a God of restoration, for his desire and ability to restore your life and relationships and all that he desires to come to pass in your life—as you fully turn to him and commit your life to him—for all to be made new.

A Life-Changing Prayer

Chapter Nine

All of you, clothe yourselves with humility toward one another, because, "God opposes the proud but gives grace to the humble." Humble yourselves, therefore, under God's mighty hand, that he may lift you up in due time.

1 PETER 5:5B–6

"I can't believe *you're* here," the elderly woman said to Kathy when she'd just walked into the lodge where their retreat was being held that September weekend in 1995. A few other women turned their backs when they saw her and didn't speak.

I just don't need this. I've got better things to do. I want to get out of this place, especially if this is how I'm going to be treated.

She hadn't wanted to come to the retreat, but her mom and a friend begged her to. If she went home, her mother would be terribly disappointed. So would the friend who had signed up to room with her.

So Kathy came. But after a few unfriendly looks from women, she started thinking again about the frustrations she had with the church.

It wasn't like she and her husband Rod were trying to cause trouble or take control. And they weren't newcomers. They'd been active in the church for two decades, ever since they'd gotten married. They showed up every Sunday. Every Wednesday. For special events and Vacation Bible Schools. They gave their time and money. They both served and led committees. Kathy played the piano on Sunday nights and taught a teenage girls' class; Rod was a deacon.

Crossing her arms, Kathy thought, *We've got a reason to complain,* as she sat on the back row waiting and the worship team started up the music. *What a rut our church is in. Rod's got so many ideas for updated, new programs to reach people. But no, it's the same old, same old. A country club instead of an outreach center. Too legalistic. Church as usual. There are so many people we could reach if only they'd be open to change.*

And the youth minister . . . that's another place that really needed a change. She, along with some other members, were unhappy with the way he ran the teen programs.

They were sick of it.

Being a concerned, strong woman, Kathy had taken the side of "against the youth minister" and spoken her mind about him whenever she got the chance. As a result, even though she and her husband felt they had good motives, they began to be viewed as troublemakers by some of the members.

Her thoughts went back to what she'd told Rod that week when the subject of church came up. "Let's just go somewhere else. There are plenty of other good churches. Things are never going to change." The truth was all their friends were here and she'd miss them if she and Rod left.

While the music started up and announcements were made, Kathy folded her hands across her chest. *I don't even know why I'm here. A movie with Rod sounds a lot better for Friday night.*

The evening dragged on.

***

Saturday, after the speaker's message, all the women were told to go outside for quiet time to listen to God.

"We crave greatness for our lives, and God asks us to become little. To pass through the door that leads to his King-dom, we must go down on our knees."

Catherine Doherty

Kathy sat alone on a quilted comforter spread over the grass. Bible propped on her lap, she was surrounded by trees beginning to turn into their fall colors. A splatter of gold leaves on one tree, yellow ones on another twirling to the ground. Normally, she didn't open her Bible except for at church or teaching the teens. But this time she had an assignment.

She looked up the first verse the speaker had given: John 3:16. *Oh, I know that verse. I memorized it as a kid.* Then something caused her to read it aloud: "For God so loved the world that he gave his one and only Son, that whoever believes in him shall not perish but have eternal life."

As she read, the truth of this verse sunk in as it never, ever had before. *God really loves me just as I am. Even when other people don't like me. With all my bad attitudes. God loves me. Just the way I am today, he died for me. He loves me.*

She hadn't understood that verse until that moment. *Here I am, thirty-eight years old, just grasping what God did for me.* She felt like a slow learner to be just realizing this when she'd been in church all her life.

Then she turned over to Revelation where the speaker had told them to read in chapter 3: "I know your deeds, that you are neither cold not hot. I wish you were either one or the other! So, because you are lukewarm—neither hot not cold—I am about to spit you out of my mouth" (vv. 15–16).

That's strange. In all the services I've been to and classes I've taught, I've never noticed that verse. I do not want God to spit me out of his mouth!

Suddenly a picture appeared in her mind's eye. She was straddling a fence. One foot was in the church, and the other foot was in the world. Though she rarely ever cried, certainly not at a church function, Kathy broke down and wept. She knew that verse was talking about her, and that she was not spiritually "hot" but rather "cold." Acting the part of a good Christian, but stagnant. Stale. Keeping up appearances but hard-hearted inside.

The next verses hit the target as well: "You say, 'I am rich. I have acquired wealth and do not need a thing'" (v. 17). It was true that she and Rod had a nice home and cars, a swimming pool, and plenty of money, and that had always made her feel special. And there was a certain pride in that.

But it was like God saw deep into her soul, calling to her, "Wake up! Listen to me!"

She realized in that moment that she had to stop sitting on the fence and make a decision—to serve God or Satan. *I'm probably not doing either of them any good. I'm just straddling them both—God's camp and the world's.*

The thought occurred to her: put God first for once. Do the simple things the speaker had told them. Read her Bible every day, first thing before all the busyness rushed in.

That morning Kathy made a vow just between herself and God.

She was going to try him. On her own, she'd see if prayer was real, if in fact God was real and would meet her and speak to her. If it didn't work, she was going to quit church and God, abandon her faith, and dive into what the world had to offer.

As the decision was made, tears began to flow uncontrollably. She felt something like refreshing water wash over her soul. It was so different from the deadness and emptiness she'd felt for so long. She didn't know what it was. But something had changed.

When the women reconvened and shared in groups what God had taught them, Kathy didn't tell anyone. Something had changed inside her. But if her friends knew, they'd give her advice or chide her if she failed. She couldn't stand that. It had to be just her and God.

***

On Monday morning Kathy came down the stairs into the light of their living room, her favorite room in the house. She put her Bible on the coffee table as a reminder of what God had laid on her heart to do, so she'd see it first thing every day. Normally when the kids left for school, she'd grab a cup of coffee and be out the door for a tennis game or call her friends and make lunch plans.

Today was different. She picked up her Bible and sat on the couch. She was determined to keep up her part of the deal.

Sure enough, God did not let her down. Like the sunshine coming through the large plate-glass windows, the Spirit came through to meet her right where she was. He began to speak to her—but not in the way she thought he would. In one of the first verses she read that morning, he pointed to a blind spot in her and her husband's lives she hadn't seen before: pride.

"Humility is a necessary prerequisite for grace. When you are humiliated, grace is on the way. . . . The humble person has changed humiliation into humility."

Bernard of Clairvaux

"All of you, clothe yourselves with humility toward one another, because 'God opposes the proud but gives grace to the humble,'" she read that first morning. "Humble yourselves, therefore, under God's mighty hand, that he may lift you up in due time" (1 Peter 5:5b–6).

Other verses followed. Day by day, everything she read pointed to pride and humility:

- "When pride comes, then comes disgrace, / but with humility comes wisdom" (Proverbs 11:2).
- "Pride only breeds quarrels, / but wisdom is found in those who take advice" (Proverbs 13:10).
- "The fear of the Lord teaches a man wisdom, / and humility comes before honor" (Proverbs 15:33).
- "Pride goes before destruction, / a haughty spirit before a fall" (Proverbs 16:18).

It was like God took a big yellow highlighter and pointed them out, showing her how little humility she and her husband had.

- "Scripture says: 'God opposes the proud, but gives grace to the humble.' Submit yourselves, then to God" (James 4:6b–7).

- "For whoever exalts himself will be humbled, and whoever humbles himself will be exalted" (Matthew 23:12).

One morning she read the story of Naaman in 2 Kings 5, the commander of an army who wanted to be healed of his leprosy. Even though Naaman was a highly ranked officer, he still had to be humble in order for God to work. She saw that obedience and humility go hand in hand.

The story in Luke 7 was the clincher. Jesus was invited to the Pharisee's home for a meal. The sinful woman comes in and her tears fall on Jesus as she anoints him with expensive perfume (vv. 37–38). Kathy wrote in the margin of her Bible: "Amazing she did that. I want to be this humble. To not care one bit who was around but just free with my Lord, to respond to him."

God couldn't have made it more clear or unmistakable. She was supposed to pray for humility for her husband and for herself.

Kneeling by the couch (because that seemed a good place to start) Kathy prayed, "Lord, your Word says you set yourself against the proud and give favor to the humble. I know we're not humble people. In fact, we're full of pride. So I pray for humility for Rod and me. I have no idea how you're going to do it, but I know this is what you're saying and I know it's what you want."

She didn't tell her husband what she was praying, but each morning she petitioned God to work in them:

"Lord, you said that pride breeds quarrels. Make us humble people who receive advice and find wisdom."

"Take away our pride and give us humble hearts that are obedient to you."

"Change Rod and me, Lord. You said that blessed are those who are meek and humble. That's sure not us."

"He that is down needs fear no fall,
He that is low, no pride;
He that is humble ever shall
have God to be His guide." *John Bunyan*

In November of that year, Kathy and Rod were sitting around a table at a local restaurant with their best friends when the topic of the congregational business meeting came up. Since their senior pastor had resigned, the Nominating Committee had met and prayed about who they thought God wanted on the Search Committee. That Wednesday night the names would be announced and voted on by the church.

"Rod, you ought to be on the committee," said Don. "You've been here longer than any of us. Besides, you're a deacon and you've served in lots of ways."

"I don't know if it'll fly, Don."

"Sure, both of you are always outside the box, but that's what we need. New people, new ideas."

"You know those folks aren't going to nominate me, especially since they want to keep the status quo." Ron replied. "Sure, I'd love to be on it. There are so many great things we could do as a church if we chose the right person, but I don't like my chances."

"I'm going to nominate you from the floor anyway," Don said.

"We'll second it," Janie and Robert agreed.

Kathy had misgivings because no one had ever questioned the

Nominating Committee. But she kept her thoughts to herself and tried to be supportive.

Two days later, members streamed in the doors to the auditorium for the Wednesday-night meeting. With the rustle of papers and sshhing of kids, the meeting started. There were no surprises on who was nominated to be on the Search Committee.

After the names were read, the chairman of the deacons said, "We're ready for a vote. All in favor, say . . ."

"Just a minute. Could I speak? I want to nominate someone for the committee, someone who deserves to be on it," said their friend Don as he stood up.

"This is highly unusual, but go ahead," the chairman responded.

"I want to nominate Rod Coleman to serve on the Search Committee. Rod and Kathy have faithfully served this church for almost twenty years. He's a great deacon and would be a valuable addition to the team that looks for a pastor."

All of a sudden things went from bad to worse. From one side of the auditorium to the other, people stood up and told all the reasons Rod didn't deserve to be on the Search Committee. How he and Kathy had brought dissension and caused trouble.

Kathy was ready to explode. It was like being on trial or, even worse, crucified. And for what? Just because her husband wanted to be on the Search Committee?

The maroon carpet and grey walls seemed to be closing in on her as embarrassment and anger mixed together. She wanted to sink through the carpet and disappear—or better yet, run out those doors all the way to China and never come back. Never have to look at these Pharisees or listen to them.

"I'm leaving," she whispered to Rod. "I've got to get out of here."

Holding her hand, he shook his head gently. He was hurting, too; she could see it in his eyes. Being on display like this made him feel like a fool, humiliated and rejected by the very people he'd served with and known for years.

"Don't dare run out of those doors. Stay," she sensed God saying.

Suddenly she remembered all those mornings she'd prayed for humility. *Oh, no. Is this the answer to my prayers? I guess I can't get out of this*, she thought.

When the meeting was finally over, Kathy's protective nature took over. Wanting to defend her husband, she walked up to the chairman of the deacons and gave him a piece of her mind. And a few other people who'd misjudged her husband. But as the couple drove home, she regretted it. *What a slow learner I am. What are you trying to say, Lord?*

Rod and Kathy sat on their living room sofa and sobbed in humiliation and embarrassment after the meeting. Their closest friends came by and cried with them. Several said they were leaving the church. "If that's how Christians treat their own, we don't want to have anything to do with them."

"There are some things I need to tell you," Kathy began when the last person had walked out the door.

"Something happened to me at the retreat in September," Kathy began as she told him about John 3:16 and Revelation 3.

"I know, honey. I could sense you were different. Softer, somehow. And you stopped griping at me when I was tired after work and didn't feel like going out and started supporting me more," Rod said.

"But what you didn't know is that I started praying for humility. Not just for me, but for you too," Kathy said through her tears. "I thought that was what God wanted for all Christians. I read it over and over in the Bible. But I had no idea what my prayers were going to do. I would have never caused this or hurt you for the world."

"Kathy, it's okay. As much as it hurts, this is what I needed," he answered. "I thought I knew how the church ought to change. If they'd just do it our way. If I could just get on the right committee, I could make it happen."

"But they treated you like you were Satan and they were angels," Kathy interrupted.

"Honey, our attitude wasn't right. No, the way they did it or what they said may not have been kind. But the truth is we *aren't* the answer to all the church's problems. We thought our ideas were the only right ideas and were operating in a lot of self-effort and pride. We may have had a good plan, but we went about it in the wrong way."

"The more humble one is at God's feet,
the more useful he is in God's hand."
Watchman Nee

As much as it pained her to hear the truth, she knew Rod was right. The next day Kathy went to the Christian bookstore by herself. Browsing in the devotional section, she ran right into a woman who'd been there at the meeting.

"I'm sorry about how you and Rod were hurt last night," she said, putting her hand on Kathy's shoulder.

All she could do was bawl like a baby. Crying in a store just wasn't her. Before, she would have been mortified if someone had seen her cry in a public place. But now she didn't care. God had touched her through the simple, compassionate words of that woman. Through the voice of the Spirit she heard him say, "I know what you went through and I love you."

In the days that followed, whenever Kathy told Rod she didn't want to stay at the church, she couldn't ever be around those people again, he said, "No, God hasn't shown me we should leave. And if we leave, a bunch of others may leave and lead to a church split. I don't think that's what God wants. We'll stay as long as he wants us to be here."

Over ten years later, Rod and Kathy are still there. From that moment on, Rod was never the same. Having experienced the power of prayer in a very personal, real way, he gave his life totally and completely to Christ. It took a while before others responded in grace to the couple and realized how they'd changed, but God had his way in this church and is still at work.

As a result of this experience, their marriage was changed. Their home was changed. No longer was it centered on success, but on Christ, and they sought his guidance often. When Rod held business meetings or company Christmas parties, he humbly opened with prayer. As their business changed, many other people outside their family were impacted as well.

Because Kathy and her husband so experienced the amazing power and blessing of prayer, she gained the vision in 1998 for a "Mom's Day of Prayer,"[2] to bring mothers together for an annual day of prayer on behalf of all children. It wasn't easy to gather women for the MDOP in her area. Some of the women who'd been involved with prayer concerts and events for years asked her, "Are you for real?" or criticized her plan.

But the criticism rolled off her back like water because all she wanted was to be like the sinful woman who had poured the perfume on Jesus' feet. She wasn't trying to impress anyone. More than anything, she wanted to be obedient.

Heart to Heart:
QUESTIONS FOR REFLECTION, DISCUSSION, AND JOURNALING

1. *The desire for renewal.* Sometimes we want to see revival in our church. We'd love to see great things happen. But it begins in the humble hearts and homes of individual believers who aren't building their hopes on their own efforts but depending on God alone. What would you like to see happen in your own church? What might he be calling you to do as part of this renewal?

2. *What should I pray?* When women ask Kathy "How can I pray for my husband?" she always answers, "Pray for humility for you and your husband," because she knows without a doubt that it changed her husband's life and their family forever. Let me encourage you to look up and reread the verses on humility throughout this chapter. Then consider: what would keep you from praying a prayer for humility?

3. *Like a child.* Madeleine L'Engle once wrote that "We can be humble only when we know that we are God's children, of infinite value and eternally loved." What qualities of a child is God working on in your life and heart?

4. Our pride often hides behind our desire to live well and place ourselves above Jesus and others. Spend a few moments asking God to reveal any hidden pride and help you to walk humbly with him and others and write it here:

5. John Piper describes five aspects of humility God tells us about in his Word: that it begins with a sense of subordination to God in Christ, that humility doesn't demand a right to better treatment than Jesus got, that it asserts truth not to control or boost our ego but to serve Christ and love others, that it realizes it is dependent on grace for all knowing and believing. And last, that humility knows it (and we) are fallible.[3] In which of these five areas do you most need to grow more humble?

Your Own Marriage Prayer

A prayer for humility is kind of like asking God to let us fellowship and share in the sufferings of Jesus (see 1 Peter 4:13) or to prune us (see John 15). We recoil from that kind of prayer because it sounds too hard. Yet the truth is humility is very important to God and it brings blessing and intimacy with him—because he hangs out with the humble but resists the proud. Before writing your prayer, read the verses in this chapter's "Glimpses of God" on the value of humility.

Glimpses of God:
Jesus Christ, Clothed in Humility

Scripture tells us that Jesus is the visible image of the invisible God: "The Son is the radiance of God's glory and the exact representation of his being, sustaining all things by his powerful word" (Hebrews 1:3).

"Because Christ came to the world clothed in humility," A.W. Tozer wrote, "he will always be found among those who are clothed with humility." In other words, God is drawn to humble people and not to those who are full of pride at how great and superior they are. The invitation to intimacy comes through humility.

Consider Jesus as you read the verses in Philippians 2:1–11 that describes his humility and how we are to live. I love the down-to-earth, practical way *The Message* renders this passage:

> If you've gotten anything at all out of following Christ, if his love has made any difference in your life, if being in a community of the Spirit means anything to you, if you have a heart, if you *care*—then do me a favor: Agree with each other, love each other, be deep-spirited friends. Don't push your way to the front; don't sweet-talk your way to the top. Put yourself aside, and help others get ahead. Don't be obsessed with getting your own advantage. Forget yourselves long enough to lend a helping hand.
> Think of yourselves the way Christ Jesus thought of himself. He had equal status with God but didn't think so much of himself that he had to cling to the

advantages of that status no matter what. Not at all.
When the time came, he set aside the privileges of
deity and took on the status of a slave, became *human*! . . . It was an incredibly humbling process. He
didn't claim special privileges. Instead, he lived a
selfless, obedient life and then died a selfless, obedient death—and the worst kind of death at that: a
crucifixion.

Now read from Isaiah and purpose to embrace a humility that will
lift you to the heavens and ever closer to God:

"The high and lofty one who inhabits eternity, the Holy One, says
this: 'I live in that high and holy place with those whose spirits are
contrite and humble. I refresh the humble and give new courage to
those with repentant hearts.'" (Isaiah 57:15 NLT)

Flight to Freedom

Chapter Ten

Do not fear, for I am with you;
do not be dismayed, for I am your God.
I will strengthen you and help you;
I will uphold you with my righteous right hand.

Isaiah 41:10

Stan and Thelma Botten approached the immigration check-out desk at Johannesburg Airport, South Africa, with their boarding passes and passports in hand. It had been a tearful good-bye with all four of their daughters and three sons-in-law and grandchildren Eugene and Lysel. Then the long drive to the airport past restaurants, schools their children had attended, parks where they'd picnicked as a family. The church they'd been married in. Corporate buildings where Stan had met in his work as an engineer, the government and defense ministry compound where he'd served as a special forces colonel in the South African military. Their hearts ached as they realized they didn't know when or if they would be back to the country where they were born and lived all of their fifty-two years.

As they patiently waited in line, the couple was filled with feelings of deep regret—and anticipation of a new beginning in a country they had only seen on television and movies. *When will we be able to see our children and grandchildren again? Will we be able to make a new life in America?*

When they presented their documents, the official carefully studied Stan's passport. "Are you Mr. Stanley Botten?" he asked.

"Yes," he answered, wondering why the man asked. Surely the official could see his name on the passport. At that moment, two stern-faced men who had been standing out from the crowd walked up to him.

"Mr. Botten, come with us. We want you to answer some questions."

Stan's mind raced. *What have I done? What do they want with me?*

The two men ushered him and his wife into a small room. In the middle of the room stood their suitcases.

"We are from the police and the commercial division and we have reason to believe you are leaving the country with a large amount of money."

"What do you mean? I have only what is normally allowed," Stan said.

"Do you mind if we search your cases?"

They began to unpack the couple's luggage in front of them, but the search turned up nothing. One of the officers exclaimed firmly, "Mr. Botten, we are taking you to Pretoria (one of the capitals of South Africa) for further questioning. We do not advise you to resist. Your wife can carry on and leave on the flight."

Stan's petite wife squared her shoulders. "I certainly will not."

The police loaded Stan into the car and set off for Pretoria Central Prison. After a call to their family, son-in-law Ferdinand took Thelma to their house.

The couple's travel plans had come to a sudden halt.

"What is this all about?" Stan asked while en route to the prison.

"You'll find out tomorrow," the policeman answered.

In a state of shock, anger, and disbelief, thoughts raced through his mind. *Why are they doing this to me? What have I done to deserve to be treated like a common criminal?*

On arrival at Pretoria Central Prison, the guards took Stan's fingerprints, removed his belt and shoelaces and processed him through the system. Another guard took his briefcase and listed all its contents. He made him sign some documents and took the briefcase away. Inside his briefcase was his high-blood-pressure medication.

The armed escorts marched him down several dark corridors lined on both sides with steel bars. Each time a steel door opened and closed, it sounded like a clap of doom.

Finally he was placed in a prison cell by himself. A feeling of foreboding came over him as his eyes took in his new home: a small, dark cell block. Hundreds of messages were scratched on the gray concrete walls. On the back wall was a small window high and out of reach. The only light was on a wall twenty feet from the cell.

The small space was bare except for a single bed covered with a rough blanket and a flat pillow. In the corner stood a bucket that served as a toilet.

Down the passage not far away, he heard loud, noisy drunkards. Pacing the floor, thoughts raced through his mind. His wife and he had made a difficult decision to leave the land they still loved and proudly served. Just as all the other men in South Africa, at the age of nineteen after two years of active duty, Stan had been allocated to a Citizen Force Regiment, where he was to serve three months a year until the age of fifty-five.

Instead of trying to fight the system or remaining a low-level private, he had volunteered for promotion training courses. From

1963 to 1968 he rose to the rank of second lieutenant. Later, in 1984, he became a commandant. He also joined a Special Forces Reconnaissance Regiment and was eventually promoted to second in command.

Stan's mind went back to a recent monthly intelligence briefing at Special Forces Headquarters. In full dress uniform, Stan had stood by as the intelligence officer informed the men their unit was being disbanded. The government was about to be overthrown, and the African National Congress (ANC) led by Nelson Mandela was expected to take over power. Mandela had recently been freed after being incarcerated for twenty-seven years for acts of terrorism. Soon he would be in charge of the entire country of South Africa—and Stan and officers who'd served alongside him would become the enemy.

In that meeting he discovered that his name and those in his Special Force's regiment were on a hit list because their assignment for several years had been to find and destroy ANC terrorist bases in Angola, Mozambique, and Zimbabwe. The very same men who would soon be in power. Unofficially, they were being told to get out of South Africa, if they had the money and skills—or face the consequences.

In addition to the impending threat on his life, the economy was taking a nosedive with 45 percent unemployment. Observing the political turmoil that was coming and economic ruin in neighboring African countries, Stan and Thelma weren't optimistic about their future. At fifty-two years old, he had only ten to fifteen years left to pursue his career.

So after much thought, he and his wife made the agonizing decision to leave behind all they had and all those they loved for America.

"Oh God, God inconceivable . . . I have erred . . . I knew that I was going astray . . . but I never forgot Thee. I always felt Thy presence even in the very moment of my sins. I all but lost Thee, but Thou hast . . . saved me!" *Leo Tolstoy*

Now he paced the floor in a twelve-by-twelve prison cell, not knowing if he'd get out alive or if they'd ever be able to leave the country. Long into the night his analytical mind began to strategize. *How am I going to get out of this situation? Who can I contact for help? What will I do?*

Suddenly he realized that he could no longer be the hero or the self-made man he'd always prided himself in being. Only with God's help could he get out of this situation.

"Stanley, you have not settled your affairs with me," he heard God say clearly in the darkness of his cell. "You need to get your life in order."

Both he and his wife gave their lives to Christ in their youth but had badly backslidden. Once they'd been active with the young people's ministry of the church. But when their children came along, they started to stray, having less and less time to go to church or even pray. They had gone their own ways and not God's way.

Although they occasionally attended the local Methodist church, they weren't committed. Their four children, his engineering career and military service, their social and community life were all of first priority and kept them very busy.

Stan knew they had strayed far from the promises they had made on their wedding day in a little Baptist church in a small town called Roodepoort on the west side of Johannesburg. And that over the years, they had grown lukewarm. It was time to seek God's counsel and not their own. He had to do something about it.

He knelt down on the dank floor and prayed for forgiveness. Only then did the anger and anxiety that had been building from the moment of arrest to being put in a prison cell begin to dissolve. Gradually a calmness came over him and he slept.

The following morning the police interrogated him and it became clear the officials were looking for something to charge him with. Stan knew the allegations they'd made so far were totally trumped up and false. Finally the public prosecutor asked him, "Mr. Botten, have you done something to upset somebody high up? I have been given strict instructions to keep you at all costs."

Later that day he appeared before the magistrate in Pretoria. The public prosecutor had told him Stan was about to flee the country and they needed more time to investigate possible embezzlement. The magistrate released him on bail of five thousand dollars and took away his passport. He told him to report to his local police station once a week and to appear before his court again in two weeks.

When reunited with his wife later that day, Thelma told him she had been praying for him and had rededicated herself to Christ while watching a Christian program on the television.

The first thing they did together was to bow their heads and pray. The next Sunday he and Thelma attended church with the encouragement of their daughter Berenice and her husband, Mark. It was a tearful, repentant man who walked down the aisle that day and rededicated his life to Christ.

From that day on, the couple was fully committed to God, and their lives began to be transformed. No longer did they figure out their plans and leave the Lord out. Now every day they started their morning with prayer, reading a daily devotional and the Bible Thelma had purchased when her husband was in prison.

One day Stan prayed, and Thelma would read aloud the passage from the Bible and the devotional. The next day they switched. If there were other needs that they felt should be covered, the other spouse would add to the prayer. Every week they had counseling with Erol, their local pastor. He prayed over them for guidance and the resolution of their situation.

As they continued to join their prayers with their pastor and family, their hearts were filled with faith and hope. In spite of all the difficulties and roadblocks, and having to appear week after week before the magistrate to be questioned, they believed that the Lord had his hand on everything that was happening to them. When he was asked questions, God gave him the words to respond. When they had fears, they remembered that God promised to be with them and strengthen them (see Isaiah 41:10), and they prayed for his help.

"When you are at the end of your rope, God is there to catch you—but not before." *Erwin W. Lutzer*

After three months and twenty thousand dollars to cover the costs of an advocate, Stan's case was transferred to their local magistrate in Kempton Park. On his first appearance before the magistrate, the public prosecutor stated they had no charges and asked for the case to be dismissed.

Now the couple was free to leave—but they had very little money. It had all been spent on lawyers. They had to get out of the country as soon as possible. So after praying about it, they decided to place all their trust in God and go to America as originally planned. They had one contact in Princeton, New Jersey, who might be able to help them, so they got tickets to New Jersey.

On Monday, they went to Pretoria to collect Stan's passport and through a contact were able to get their tickets renewed for the earliest flight on Wednesday, July 22, 1992.

With a lot less ceremony than the first time, they said good-bye to daughters, sons-in-law, and grandchildren. Fearful of what had happened the last time they attempted to leave South Africa, they quickly boarded the aircraft for America. As the plane filled up with passengers, the two buckled their seat belts and held hands. Thelma was in tears and Stan's head was about to explode with the tension, anxiety, and fatigue from the past harrowing months.

They had had to leave everything behind—besides their precious loved ones, they said good-bye to friends, family treasures and antiques, reputation and career, their home, and all they'd worked for their whole lives. Starting over at age fifty-two would be difficult. They didn't know anyone in the whole U.S. continent and had only one phone number for a possible job in New Jersey.

Yet as the plane rose and the brilliance of the rising sun shone through the windows, they relaxed and took deep breaths. The couple knew they had with them the most important thing of all—their faith in Christ. They had no idea of their future in America, only the knowledge that God had paved the way and that he held the future.

After arriving in the States and calling their New Jersey contact, they were told he would not be able to offer Stan employment but that he knew of someone in Houston, Texas, who might need an engineer with special qualifications in the field of nondestructive testing, which is what Stan's background was in.

By the time they got on the flight for Houston, they had very little money left. They arrived at Houston International Airport with a telephone number, three hundred dollars in their pockets, and faith that the Lord was with them and would supply all their needs. They booked a room in a small hotel near the airport.

The next morning Stan made the all-important phone call and was asked to come in for an interview. During the meeting he presented all his qualifications and experience to the divisional manager of a large inspection company and was told they would contact him later. The next morning he received an offer for a three-month contract. He'd be paid twenty dollars an hour plus half the car rental and half their hotel bill for the first week. The company would assist in finding an apartment for which they'd pay half.

Needless to say, Stan accepted. Before the three-month period ended, he was offered a more permanent position with another company as vice president of Industrial Services.

After ten years, God has blessed Thelma and Stan with a beautiful home and a senior position in the company they first visited when they arrived in the U.S.

And after fourteen years, on March 29, 2006, they gained their American citizenship.

Two of their daughters remained in South Africa with their husbands and children, one daughter and her husband moved to Australia, and one daughter lives with her husband and children in Arizona.

Though their family is spread all across the world, God has given them a spiritual family in the First Baptist Church in Houston, Texas. From the pastor and staff to every member of the congregation, they have embraced the Bottens like one of the family. They have invited them to Fourth of July parties and Thanksgiving and Christmas celebrations and everything in between. When Stan's mother died and he could not go to the funeral and when their daughter Cheryl got married back in South Africa and only Thelma could go since Stan would still be in danger if he returned, their choir friends were there for them with comfort and encouragement.

And the day they became American citizens, many of their forever family was there to cheer them on and celebrate with parties and special events.

> "In confession . . . we open our lives to healing, reconciling, restoring, uplifting grace of him who loves us in spite of what we are." *Louis Cassels*

They give all their thanks and glory to their heavenly Father, who promised to strengthen them and help them, to take care of them as they place their trust and faith in him. He is the one who meets them every morning as they read his word and pray together, just as they have for the last fourteen years.[1]

Heart to Heart:

QUESTIONS FOR REFLECTION, DISCUSSION, AND JOURNALING

1. *A life of faith.* Stan and Thelma's experience in coming to America beautifully illustrates the true meaning of living a life of faith. Once they turned from taking care of everything on their own (without God's help) to trusting him with their future, their faith was renewed and their lives transformed. What do you face in your life and/or your marriage that currently tests your faith in God?

2. Scripture says, "Without faith it is impossible to please God" (Hebrews 11:6) and also teaches that if we have faith as small as a mustard seed, then we can tell our mountains of fear, worry, disbelief, control, and anxiety to move on (see Matthew 17:20). Keeping your own mountains in mind, how might you better demonstrate your faith to God?

3. *Finding freedom.* This couple's flight to freedom wasn't only a physical one, because they had come into freedom in Christ through their adversities. How would you describe your personal journey to freedom in the midst of adversity? What would you like to see or feel?

4. *Getting personal with God.* Stan and Thelma surrendered their life to God when they both (individually) were made aware they had been living complacent, compromising lives. They admitted to having backslidden in their personal walk with Christ and turned from their lukewarm ways, and began seeking him together. How could something you learn in this story apply to your own life?

Your Own Marriage Prayer

Maybe you're facing a very difficult time in your life and you are not certain of your future, or even your today. Your spouse may not be in a literal prison as Stan was when he had a life-changing encounter with Christ. But he or she may be in a prison of depression, a valley of fear, or going through a wilderness season. Using the key verse for this chapter, pray God's promises of his faithfulness for your marriage:

Glimpses of God: A God of Faithfulness

God is faithful! Say that aloud, will you? *God is faithful!* Deuteronomy 7:9 says, "Know therefore that the LORD your God is God; he is the faithful God." First Corinthians 1:9 says, "God, who has called you into fellowship with his Son Jesus Christ our Lord, is faithful." As the hymn goes, "Great is his faithfulness!"

God delights in showing his faithfulness in our lives because it is the essence of who he is. But he also delights in enabling us to live a life of faithfulness to him. Read Hebrews 11, which is sometimes referred to as the Hall of Faith chapter since it commends the ancients for their enduring faith in God. What is the beginning point for our living in faith? It is committing our all to God, believing him, and trusting in his faithfulness no matter what we face. Let me encourage you to meditate on God's faithfulness as you read these verses:

- Deuteronomy 7:9
- Deuteronomy 32:4
- Psalm 89:8
- Psalm 143:1
- 2 Thessalonians 3:3
- Hebrews 10:23
- 1 Thessalonians 5:24

The Best Is Yet To Be

Chapter Eleven *We do not know what to do, but our eyes are upon you.*

2 CHRONICLES 20:12B

The old black Blazer sped along, packed with Holmes and me, our two teenage boys and twelve-year-old daughter, plus our sheltie, Lady. Driving down the Pennsylvania turnpike, we were moving from Maine back to our home state of Oklahoma.

Our first stop had been in Connecticut two nights before, where we had dinner with Clara and Rich Ruffin. The Ruffins were new friends we'd met a few months before when I'd spoken for the Educators' Conference in Hartford. Having lived in the spiritual desert of the beautiful state of Maine for a year and a half, we'd been hungry for Christian fellowship. So taking a small detour through Connecticut before we headed south was worth it to see Clara and Rich. Being with them was like a breath of fresh air, and the savory roast, baked potatoes, and chocolate cake, mixed with the warm hospitality of their home, gave us a good start for the long trip ahead.

Now an icy February rain was drenching the highways. Fog was making it hard to see. It was only three in the afternoon, but the traffic was fierce, and we were already weary from the days and days of packing and two nights on the road. Every time we stopped for gas and Lady jumped out to go to the bathroom, she got wet all over again. A wretched, damp doggy smell permeated the car. Our long-legged sons and daughter with their backpacks of books and stuff crowded each other's space in the backseat.

I turned around and saw Justin's crestfallen face looking out the window, probably thinking about his car, which we'd had to leave behind. I was thinking about it, too.

As he'd caravanned behind us, his 1980 gold, much-loved Chevette had broken down on the turnpike. We'd had it towed to a service station but were told it needed a new engine and transmission. Since that would cost way more money than we could afford, we had to leave his car behind, selling it for salvage. We packed the clothes and belongings that were in his car in UPS boxes, mailed them on to Oklahoma City, and continued on our journey.

Just another thing we lost in Maine, I thought. Our savings when the stock market crashed and real estate prices plummeted the month we arrived, our house in Oklahoma City when the man renting it during our absence sent so many insufficient funds to the bank they'd foreclosed on the house. And our family car that had been hit head-on by a Grateful Dead groupie on the way to a concert months before, burning and totaling the vehicle.

"Not many people take three cars to Maine and come back with only one," I quietly remarked to Holmes. Immediately I regretted saying it when I saw his jaw clench.

That's how our "adventure" in Maine had been—full of trials, unexpected downturns, and struggles. A character-building experience.

"God is never in a panic, nothing can be
done that he is not absolute Master of,
and no one in earth or heaven can shut
a door he has opened, nor open a door

> he has shut. God alters the inevitable
> when we get in touch with him."
> *Oswald Chambers*

But I had to keep my attitude up for the sake of Holmes and the children and think about the good things that had come out of our time in Yarmouth during the last year and a half. And there had been plenty of those. I mentally started rehearsing them: the family times we'd had that cost next to nothing, like riding bikes on the island next to Yarmouth, picnicking on Sunday after church, cross-country skiing in the woods behind our house, the learning experiences each of the kids had in a small-town school.

Alison must have heard my comment to Holmes. "But Mom, just as soon as Dad starts the Harris' house, we'll be able to get another car!" she said hopefully. "Could we stop at McDonald's for dinner?"

That was our expectation. Not a Happy Meal but a happy job for Holmes. And the reason why we were moving back—for my husband to resume his custom-building career. Things appeared promising if he could start the house that was scheduled.

The Harrises had purchased one of the remaining lots in the New England-style neighborhood in Quail Creek where Holmes had built homes a few years before. Emily and Ian had flown him back to Oklahoma to meet with them so he could begin designing their dream home. They loved the plans he drew up and seemed ready to go. So, turning down the job L.L. Bean had offered him, we'd packed everything up, called the moving truck, and headed south. The kids were looking forward to getting back to the schools and friends they'd left. And Holmes was excited about breaking ground and starting construction on the Harris' new house soon after our arrival.

Things were looking up!

The sun was shining brightly on the day we moved into the leased house Holmes had found for us on his trip back a month before. Amidst the unpacking and picture-hanging, Holmes called Emily and Ian to get together and finalize the plan so he could take it down to the courthouse for the city's approval.

Strangely, they didn't return his calls. A few days went by, then a week. Still he heard nothing from his clients.

"Maybe they're out of town, honey," I encouraged. "Or just busy? They sure seemed in a hurry to get you back and start this house when we were up there in Maine!"

Ten days later when Holmes and his clients finally met to pore over the plans for their new house and set the date to break ground—or so he thought—Ian leveled with him:

"Holmes, we really like what you've designed. This is just exactly what we want in a house. But we need to tell you that you can't start construction until our grandmother passes away and we get our inheritance. She's been ill and was in the hospital a few months ago but she's rallied and gone back to the assisted living center."

After Holmes mentally picked himself up off the ground, his thoughts raced. *Why didn't they tell me this before we drove almost two thousand miles across the country from Maine? Where can I get a construction job on short notice? What are we going to do in the meantime?* He certainly didn't wish for the quick demise of the grandma, but to say this put his building company and family in a difficult situation was an understatement.

No matter what I said or how I tried to encourage Holmes in the days that followed, his stress grew by the day . . . and sometimes by the hour. Although rent and utilities were paid up until the first of the month, what were we going to do after that? There were groceries to buy, gasoline and the kids' needs being back in school, etc.

Within a few weeks our money ran out. There wasn't a family member we could borrow from. We couldn't get a loan from the bank without secure employment. I was working as a freelance writer but that income was definitely "chicken today and feathers tomorrow"—and I seemed to be in a season of feathers. That wouldn't buy any groceries or pay any of the bills, which began stacking up on the kitchen counter.

Holmes and I were saying our individual "Help, God!" prayers, but one night around midnight, both from anxiety and a long day, we collaborated. We knelt by the bed, leaning our heads on the comforter, and prayed together.

"Lord, we've trusted you with our lives and our future. We've given you our family and all that we are," I began. "We prayed long and hard about going to Maine and asked your guidance, and things didn't work out as we'd planned. But you've provided for us to get back here and we're up against a serious problem. Holmes has no work and needs a job. We just don't know what to do . . ."

I trailed off. I was telling God things he already knew and being long-winded as usual (which, actually, I don't think he minded because he loves to hear from his children just as we love to hear from our kids when they are far away).

"Lord, we really don't know what to do, but our eyes are on you. We look to you to guide us and provide," Holmes said, praying what we called the "Jehoshaphat Prayer." (A man of few words, he always got right to the point.) "Help us to know which way to go and to trust you in this stressful time."

> "God is so good that he only awaits our desire to overwhelm us with the gift of himself." *Francois Fenelon*

Falling into bed a few minutes later, we figured it was unlikely the Harrises would call in the morning with another plan of funding their new house, but we had turned to God together, entrusted our needs to him, and that was enough.

We also decided to add fasting (giving up food to concentrate on God and prayer) to our petitions for the next three days and seek God and pray together at night before bed.

Nothing changed in our circumstances. I had redone Holmes' résumé and he was spending hours each day looking for an interim job until the building project could start. While Justin, Chris, and Alison were at school each day I worked on articles on my computer. I amassed a few rejection slips and got an occasional acceptance (with payment not until publication—which meant six to nine months away). Plus I accepted a job as a Writer-in-the-Schools in a city arts program, which would start in September. That seemed a long time to wait.

Lord, we don't know what to do, but our eyes are on you.

One day in the first week of March, I looked in the refrigerator to get out turkey, cheese, and fixings for sandwiches for lunch. It was clear our provisions were getting lean. I had a dried piece of bread with peanut butter and went back to my work.

When he came home from picking the kids up at school, I asked, "Holmes, do you have any cash I could go to the grocery store with?"

A few minutes later he brought out his gallon Ozarka jug filled with change and set it on the dining room table. His eyes were lowered and stress showed in every line on his face. Slowly, quietly, Holmes began to count out dimes, quarters, and nickels, rolling them in bank papers.

Our sixteen-year-old cringed as he passed the table on his way out to shoot baskets with his brother. But change was what we had for that day—and as far as we knew, for the near future.

Suddenly the doorbell rang. It was the postman with a special delivery letter postmarked from Connecticut. The letter read: "Dear Holmes and Cheri: When we were praying, we felt the Lord impress on us to send you this check for $1,000. Maybe it is timely. We hope so. We also pray God's blessing on you and your three children in the days ahead. Love, Clara and Rich Ruffin."

Tears formed in my eyes and I looked over at Holmes, who was silent yet misty-eyed as well. Awestruck and humbled, waves of holy gratitude we could barely express in that moment swept through both of us. The same God who cares for the birds of the air and clothes the flowers of the fields (I'd just read that in the Bible) had heard our late-night prayers and seen our situation. Through that check and letter he was saying to us, "Trust me. I know your needs before you do, and I am your Provider." He just used the Ruffin's hands and feet to deliver his message and help.

"Chris! Justin! Look what came in the mail!" Ali called out the door when she saw the check. Not quite as excited as their sister, her brothers came in from the driveway basketball game and we shared the letter aloud to them.

As we thought about that miraculous day, we realized Holmes and I were not the only ones who had been praying. So was a couple almost two thousand miles away, public school teachers who weren't people of great means but who were willing to listen and obey. That provision saw us through for the next few weeks and gave us hope while Holmes was interviewing for a job at a men's clothing store until he could resume custom building.

Our financial problems didn't disappear overnight. Holmes didn't get to start a house for a year (and it wasn't even the Harrises; that was eighteen months away). We had suffered huge financial losses in the past three years and it took us a long time to recover. We drove an old (I mean ancient) white Chevrolet for a time and were grateful Grandpo gave it to us! We made our share of mistakes along the way and continued to ask, "Teach us to pray," "Help us to be good stewards." And especially, "Lord, we don't know what to do, but our eyes are on you." Our financial life has been a work-in-progress and we're still under construction.

I can't tell you we slid into a season of great prosperity after we experienced God's provision during our "change on the dining room table" experience. In fact, since we told God we'd do and go wherever he needed us in 1976, we've never had financial security and lived very few years with a set salary. We've had a few other times of counting change on the table. But in our struggles, the Lord has been our great reality, our constant Source.

"God is most glorified when we are most satisfied in Him." *John Piper*

We only stayed in that leased house two years. We moved again . . . and again, and again. But in the process of learning to depend on God in the material realm, of being a "tentmaker" to support the ministry of Families Pray USA he's entrusted to me, the Lord has drawn us closer to himself.

Whenever we've had to move, he has said over and over, "I am your Dwelling Place"—for he knows I'm a real nester by heart who'd love to get comfy in one house forever. He's reminded me, "I *am* your place of security and significance, not a physical house on this earth or a big bank account."

God has shown up time and again as our Provider, our Jehovah Jireh, who is always faithful, even if it's in the eleventh hour. As our Good Shepherd who directs and guides us. He has blessed us with three marvelous children who are now adults and praying parents themselves. They, their spouses, and our grandchildren are some of our greatest earthly gifts, far better than silver or gold.

Along the way, God has taken us to places we'd never dreamed of to minister to people in Thailand, Singapore, Switzerland, Zambia, and South Africa—and done more than we could have asked or thought.

That's why we know the words on a small pillow that has sat on our bed for several decades are true: *"The best is yet to be."*

And that forever house? It's waiting for me in heaven.

And I won't ever have to pack again!

Heart to Heart:

QUESTIONS FOR REFLECTION, DISCUSSION, AND JOURNALING

1. Joining our hearts to pray the Jehoshaphat Prayer helped Holmes and me avoid blaming each other ("Why didn't you take that job L.L. Bean offered you instead of bringing us back here to more uncertainty?" or "Why don't you get a job instead of pursuing writing when it's not bringing in much income?") or letting the problem become a wedge between us during a crushing and difficult time. By praying together, we were inviting Jesus to be the "third strand" (see Ecclesiastes 4:12) who held us together when we were stressed. In prayer, we both felt supported by God and each other as we waited for an answer and provision.

Jehoshaphat had his own incredible experience with holy support. Read 2 Chronicles 20 and write what the Lord said and did in response to Jehoshaphat's Prayer:

2. *Did your plans go south?* Maybe, like we experienced, there was (or is) a time when your expectations were met with disappointment. The plans (for a job, a new career, a move) evaporated, and you have financial or other struggles. Write here what your greatest need is:

3. *What are your biggest gaps?* Perhaps your need isn't in the material or financial area, but a need for friends, for joy to be restored to your life, for new purpose or direction—or for wisdom to use the money you do have. Maybe you are in a health crisis and long for restored strength or better healthcare (we've been there). If Jesus were sitting right beside you, what would you ask him for today— for yourself or someone you love?

4. How can you see God's answer to larger desires of your heart— joy, peace, life, or intimacy with him—even while the financial turnaround or answer to your immediate problem hasn't come?

5. How have you experienced the reality of God's presence in your situation? In our own experience, as we focused on God ("Our eyes are upon you"), he showed us he was our provider, our Shepherd who guided us, and our dwelling place. How has the Lord revealed himself to you in the midst of your situation and marriage?

6. How has God responded to your prayers for blessing and life even in the midst of *waiting* for the answer to your prayers? (Making a list of how he has been caring for you even in little ways, providing for you, sustaining you, and drawing you to himself is helpful in this process.)

Your Own Marriage Prayer

Is there a part of your life together that you are clueless about what to do with next? Perhaps you've planned and tried, but things didn't work out the way you'd hoped. Let me encourage you to pray the Jehoshaphat Prayer. It is a powerful prayer of relinquishing our own way of handling things and turning to God alone for his way, his provision, and his guidance. I believe as you do, you'll find that praying this way in the midst of a stressful situation helps you bond together instead of growing farther apart because of the stress of the situation.

Glimpses of God: The Lord Our Provider

One of the important glimpses of God we gained through this experience was that God is our provider. Genesis 22 is the first time in the Bible that God is referred to as *Jehovah Jireh*, the Lord our Provider. Read the story of Abraham and Isaac on Mt. Moriah when Abraham is about to offer his beloved son to God in obedience to him. At the moment when he has in his hand the knife and the fire, God provides a ram for sacrifice. After God provided the ram for the burnt offering, Abraham called the name of that place, "The Lord Will Provide," or *Jehovah-Jireh* (v. 14 NASB).

As Corrie ten Boom said, no matter what happens or how desperate the need, "There's no panic in heaven."[1] Throughout the history of God, he provides for his people—manna in the desert, strength in battle, protection in the lion's den—until in his provision through the life and death of Jesus, he gives us the ultimate gift: his only son, our salvation and our life. Think about how God has revealed himself to you and your family as the Lord Our Provider.

A Last Word to Readers

In the stories you've read, you've seen that when you love your spouse through prayer, your marriage is enriched—and that some marriages are marvelously transformed. When you pray as a couple, the benefits are real and lasting. As Art Hunt said, "When we share this prayer relationship as a couple, intimacy is measured not with a teaspoon—but with a shovel!"[1] With every prayer you grow toward spiritual closeness, which ripples out into your communication, friendship, and other areas of your life.

But if your spouse isn't eager to have prayer time with you or isn't connecting with God at all, don't be discouraged! Your prayers can be a great blessing for your marriage and mate. As you've seen in this book, by seeking God and loving your spouse through prayer, you can be the catalyst for change and newness of life in your marriage. You and I can't change our husbands' or wives' hearts, but God can, and his heart-changing power is released *when you pray*.

My hope and prayer is that in reading these stories and reflecting on, journaling, and discussing the questions, you've gained a vision for how prayer—and especially praying God's Word—can not only strengthen and rejuvenate your marriage, but be a vehicle for having a positive, loving, influence on your mate's days and an eternal impact as well.

As you've written your own marriage prayers in the chapters and as you persevere in these petitions until the answer comes, I encourage you to jot in the margins ways that God works in the weeks and months ahead.

And long after you've closed the pages of this book, I pray you'll remember not only the stories, verses, and principles you learned, but aspects of God's very character that these stories revealed: That he is a God of second chances, and that when you (or your spouse) have blown it and need a second, or third, or fourth chance, he is waiting for you with his unlimited resources in Christ. That he is a God of affection who loves you and your mate with an everlasting, unconditional, affectionate love which is available through prayer. That when your marriage or life is in need of restoration—whether it's affection or joy, purpose or hope—the Lord is more than able to provide; he can rekindle you and when you give him the situation or problem through prayer, you'll know you are inviting his grace, power, and restoration into your marriage. That God wants to bless you and your marriage and mate; he is a gracious God who longs to show His goodness and mercy to you. That when you have no idea what to do next or you've done all you can do and things are still a mess, you can be honest about it and pray, "Lord, we don't know what to do, but our eyes are upon you," and find him faithful again and again. He can be trusted and his promises stand forever.

As Jim Burns said in his book, *Creating An Intimate Marriage*, "There is a spiritual battle that takes place for the soul of every marriage."[2] Yet God has not left us without weapons and resources. Second Corinthians 10:4 says the weapons of our warfare in this and every battle we face on this earth are "divinely powerful." They are the Word of God and prayer—not worldly weapons but mighty weapons that bring his deliverance, protection, and help in time of need. As you continue to pray God's Word, it will bring transformation to your spiritual life and your marriage. And just as we have, you'll find you'll never run out of blessings and promises to pray into your spouse's, your children's, and your own life.

To jumpstart this process, I've included topical prayers for your marriage and mate in the next section. May they be a blessing to you and your family!

Topical Prayers for Your Marriage and Mate

Following are some of the scriptural prayers Holmes and I have found helpful in our marriage. Praying scriptural blessings is part of our privilege as believers to bless others—especially those closest to us, in our own homes. If one of the prayers below seems to hit the target, you might add it to your petitions. Most of all, I hope these prayers encourage and remind you that as you read God's Word day by day, he will highlight many prayers that will enrich and revive your marriage and spouse. Ask the Lord: *lead me to the passages that will speak to our life and marriage.* He delights to answer with his Word, which will be fresh manna for your own situations and challenges.

A Godward Focus

Lord, be the glory and lifter of our heads and hearts. Lift up our eyes to you, to focus on you, knowing that whatever happens, you are sufficient, you are enough, you are faithful. May we have a Godward focus instead of being focused on ourselves or our problems (see Psalm 3:3, Psalm 8).

Perspective

Lord, teach us to number our days that we might present to you a heart of wisdom. Help us understand how brief life is, and show us what really matters so we won't squander our time on worthless or meaningless pursuits (see Psalm 90:12).

Affection and Honor

Empower us to love each other with a genuine affection and delight in honoring each other (see Romans 12:10).

A Good Listener

Lord, help me be slow to speak, quick to listen, and slow to anger (see James 1:19).

Through Eyes of Faith

Father, help us see each other through eyes of faith and give us the grace to respond to each other as the new creations in Christ that we are instead of reacting to each other's old natures. Help us to treat each other with consideration and respect as heirs together of the grace of life (see 1 Peter 3:7, 8–12).

Faithfulness

Gracious Father, help us be faithful in little things so we will grow to be faithful in larger matters. Teach us to be good stewards of all things you've entrusted to us (see Luke 16:10).

Trust Instead of Worry

Grant us grace to trust you and to pray instead of worrying and being anxious. Teach me day by day to cast all my cares, burdens, and anxieties upon you, because you care for us affectionately and watchfully. (see Philippians 4:6, 1 Peter 5:7)

Enjoyment

Show us how to enjoy each other, not just to endure or survive in the relationship you've given us (see 1 Peter 3:2).

Provision

Thank you that you know our needs and care for us every day. As we give to others and seek your kingdom, we trust you to supply all our needs from your glorious riches which have been given to us in Christ Jesus (see Matthew 6:28–33, Philippians 4:19).

The Love That Covers

Lord Jesus, grant me the love that covers a multitude of sins. Fill me with your unfailing love for my spouse, which is inexhaustible and never runs out (see 1 Peter 4:8, Psalm 103).

Change of Heart

Father, if my mate has strayed from the truth or become captive in sin, please change his/her heart. Turn him/her from darkness into your marvelous light. May he/she come to his/her senses, escape the devil's trap, and be restored (see 2 Timothy 2:23–26).

Spiritual Awakening

I pray that the eyes of my mate's heart may be enlightened, that you would give us both a spirit of wisdom and revelation in the knowledge of Jesus, so that we may know what is the hope of your calling, the riches of the glory of your inheritance in the saints, and the surpassing greatness of your power toward us who believe (see Ephesians 1:17–18).

Grace

Father, your Word says you are able to make all grace abound. Please show me today in real ways how to lavish your grace on others, beginning with my mate (see 2 Corinthians 9:8, 2 Corinthians 12:9).

Guidance: The Jehoshaphat Prayer

Father, we don't know what to do but our eyes are upon you! Show us what to do and guide us with your hand upon us. Fill us with the knowledge of your will so we can walk in a way that pleases you (see 2 Chronicles 20, Colossians 1:9–10).

A Clean Heart

Create in me a clean heart toward my mate and everyone in my life, past and present; renew a right spirit within me (see Psalm 51:10).

Joy

Restore our joy together and our joy in life and salvation. May your joy be our strength and may our joy be full (see Nehemiah 8:10, John 15:11).

A Fruitful Life

May we not turn our hearts away from you and trust human strength or help, but trust in you, Lord, and make you our hope and confidence. May we be like trees planted along a riverbank, with roots that reach deep into the water and leaves that stay green, and may we never stop producing fruit (see Jeremiah 17:5–8, Psalm 1).

Hope

I pray that God, the source of all hope, will fill us completely with joy and peace because we trust in him. May we then overflow with confident hope through the power of the Holy Spirit (see Romans 15:13).

Parenting

Help and empower us through your power and wisdom to be the parents our kids need at each stage of their lives, to influence them for Christ, and be good role models of faithful, vibrant living (see Ephesians 6:4, Proverbs 20:7).

Love

Make our love for one another and for all people grow and overflow, just as our love for you, Lord, grows. May we live deeply in and through Christ's love (see 1 Thessalonians 3:12–13, Ephesians 3:14–21).

Encouragement

Father, you tell us over and over in your word to encourage others. Make me an encourager to my spouse and people inside our home and in the world around us, especially when they are discouraged (see 2 Corinthians 7:6, Hebrews 10:25).

God's Workmanship

May we walk in the good works and plans that you, God, prepared beforehand—for we are your workmanship, created in Christ Jesus for those very good works (see Ephesians 2:10)!

God's Glory

Father, glorify yourself and your name through our marriage. Bind our hearts together as one heart so we can live in harmony. May we be one even as you and your son are one and our home be a lighthouse to shed your love and truth to our children, family, friends, neighbors, and a watching world (see John 17:20–23).

About the Author

Cheri Fuller is an international speaker and award-winning author of over thirty books with combined sales of over one million, including *A Busy Woman's Guide to Prayer*, *A Fresh Vision of Jesus*, *The One Year Book of Praying Through the Bible*, *When Mothers Pray*, *The Mom You're Meant to Be*, and *The School Savvy Kids Series*. She has written hundreds of articles for *Family Circle*, *Focus on the Family*, *Guideposts*, and other publications and she is a contributing writer for *Today's Christian Woman* and her eNewsletter "Heart to Heart with Cheri Fuller." She has also been a frequent guest on national radio and TV programs including *Focus on the Family*, *Family Life Today*, *The 700 Club*, and many others.

Cheri's retreats and conferences for women are popular throughout the United States and overseas as she communicates a vision of the great gift, invitation, and power of prayer, and how we can connect with God in the midst of our busy lives. Her ministry, Families Pray USA, inspires and equips women, children, teens, families, and churches to impact their world through prayer.

Cheri's website, www.CheriFuller.com, features her monthly column, "Mothering By Heart," a free Bible study on prayer, and other resources on prayer and inspiration. For more information on resources or scheduling for speaking engagements or conferences, write to her at cheri@cherifuller.com.

Notes

Prayer: The Best Love Language of All

1. John Piper, *Pierced By the Word* (Sisters, OR: Multnomah Publishers, 2003), 32.
2. Madame Guyon, *Experiencing God through Prayer* (New Kensington, PA: Whitaker House, 1984), 17.
3. Jennifer Kennedy Dean, *Heart's Cry: Principles of Prayer* (Birmingham, AL: New Hope Publishers, 1992), 60.
4. Dr. James Dobson, *Love for a Lifetime* (Sisters, OR: Multnomah Publishers, 1997).
5. Oswald Chambers, "Witness of the Spirit," *My Utmost for His Highest* (Uhrichsville, OH: Barbour Publishing, 2006).
5. From a sermon by Jack Arrington, Tomball Baptist Church, Tomball, Texas.

Chapter One

1. Brent W. Bost, MD, *The Hurried Woman Syndrome* (New York: McGraw Hill, 2005), 3–5.
2. David and Claudia Arp, *10 Great Dates Before You Say I Do, 10 Great Dates to Energize Your Marriage, 10 Great Dates for Empty Nesters* (Grand Rapids, MI: Zondervan Publishers).

Chapter Two

1. Harold S. Kushner, "The Gift of Gratitude," *Family Circle*, September 2, 2003, 54.

2. Greg Smalley, "The Marriage You've Always Dreamed Of," *Marriage Partnership*, summer, 2006, 24.

3. R. A. Torrey, *How to Pray* (Springdale, PA: Whitaker House, 1983), 60–61.

Chapter Three

1. Cyndi Lamb Curry, *Keeping Your Kids Afloat When You Feel Like You're Sinking* (Ventura, CA: Regal Gospel Light, 2002).

2. Daniel Ortega and Melodie Fleming, "Declarations: Transforming Your Pain into Peace" (unpublished manuscript printout), 7.

Chapter Four

1. Eggerichs, *Love and Respect*, 67.

Chapter Six

1. A. Wetherell Johnson, "Abraham's Test and Sarah's Death," series 1, lesson 19 (Colorado Springs: International Bible Society, 1984), 1.

2. Larry Crabb, *The Papa Prayer: The Prayer You've Never Prayed* (Nashville, TN: Integrity Publishers, 2006), 31.

Chapter Seven

1. Dr. Emerson Eggerichs, *Love and Respect* (Brentwood, TN: Integrity Media, Inc., 2004), 300.

Chapter Eight

1. Sam Storms, "God's Greatest Joy," *Pray!*, May/June 2005, 8.

2. Crabb, *The Papa Prayer*, 180.

Chapter Nine

1. John Piper, *Pierced By the Word* (Sisters, OR: Multnomah Publishers, 2003), 36–37.
2. After first uniting women from different denominations, races, and backgrounds in her own Arkansas city, the Mom's Day of Prayer has spread around the world from the U.S. to Australia to Africa. Visit *www.momsdayofprayer.com* for testimonials, photos, and more information on how to bring it to your community.
3. John Piper, *Pierced by the Word*, 16.

Chapter Ten

1. Adapted from a story by Stanley Botten

Chapter Eleven

1. Corrie ten Boom, *Reflections of God's Glory* (Grand Rapids, MI: Zondervan, 1999), 92.

A Last Word to Readers

1. Art Hunt, *Praying With the One You Love* (Sisters, OR: Multnomah Publishers, 1996), 35.
2. Jim Burns, *Creating an Intimate Marriage* (Minneapolis: Bethany House Publishers, 2006), 159.

THE BOOK CLUB FOR TODAY'S CHRISTIAN FAMILY

A Letter to Our Readers

Dear Reader:

In order that we might better contribute to your reading enjoyment, we would appreciate your taking a few minutes to respond to the following questions. When completed, please return to the following:

Andrea Doering, Editor-in-Chief
Crossings Book Club
401 Franklin Avenue, Garden City, NY 11530

You can post your review online! Go to www.crossings.com and rate this book.

Title _____ Author _____

1 Did you enjoy reading this book?

❑ Very much. I would like to see more books by this author!

❑ I really liked_____

❑ Moderately. I would have enjoyed it more if_____

2 What influenced your decision to purchase this book? Check all that apply.

      ❑ Cover
      ❑ Title
      ❑ Publicity
      ❑ Catalog description
      ❑ Friends
      ❑ Enjoyed other books by this author
      ❑ Other _____

3 Please check your age range:

      ❑ Under 18   ❑ 18-24
      ❑ 25-34   ❑ 35-45
      ❑ 46-55   ❑ Over 55

4 How many hours per week do you read? _____

5 How would you rate this book, on a scale from 1 (poor) to 5 (superior)?
_____

Name_____

Occupation_____

Address_____

City_____ State_____ Zip_____